# THE
# SECURE
# CHILD

OTHER BOOKS BY STANLEY I. GREENSPAN, M.D.

# THE
# SECURE
# CHILD

*Helping Our Children*
*Feel Safe and Confident*
*in a Changing World*

STANLEY I. GREENSPAN

*A Merloyd Lawrence Book*

**DA CAPO PRESS**

A Member of the Perseus Books Group

Many of the designations used by manufacturers and sellers to distinguish their products are claimed as trademarks. Where those designations appear in this book and Da Capo Press was aware of a trademark claim, the designations have been printed in initial capital letters.

Cataloging-in-Publication data is available from the Library of Congress.

First Da Capo Press paperback edition 2003
ISBN 0-7382-0816-7

Published by Da Capo Press
A Member of the Perseus Books Group
http://www.dacapopress.com

Da Capo Press books are available at special discounts for bulk purchases in the United States by corporations, institutions, and other organizations. For more information, please contact the Special Markets Department at the Perseus Books Group, 11 Cambridge Center, Cambridge, MA 02142, or call (800) 255-1514 or (617) 252-5298, or e-mail j.mccrary@perseusbooks.com.

Text design by *Brent Wilcox*
Set in 11-point New Caledonia by the Perseus Books Group

1 2 3 4 5 6 7 8 9 10—06 05 04 03

To Nancy, Elizabeth, Jake, and Sarah

# CONTENTS

# Introduction

THROUGHOUT THE CENTURIES, THE FIRST AND FOREMOST job of parents has always been to protect their children from the dangers of the world outside the home. While recent events have compelled all families to live with a greater sense of uncertainty and stress, the task of helping children to develop the abilities they require to feel secure and grow to adulthood with confidence is not a new one. Many of the threats, as well as the ways children are exposed to danger and violence, however, are new. School violence, as well as environmental hazards and the way they are portrayed on television and other media, create fears in children that can lead to deep insecurity. Such concerns can be overwhelming to most of us, but they are especially so for children who tend to personalize events and can't yet put things in perspective. It's not unusual for young children to believe that something will happen to them or to their families simply because it has happened to someone else.

To help children feel more secure in the short run, I lay out some basic principles in this book that can enable children to cope with frightening events. These principles grow from the understanding that children's sense of security is mostly founded on their relationships with their parents and family. Family relationships are, as they have always been, a protective shield to the world, giving children the sense that the shelter of their immediate surroundings—the moment-to-moment sense of being cared for, nurtured, and protected—is in place. This provides a safe haven for children from which to explore and express their feelings, while putting frightening events in context, rather than overly personalizing them.

In addition to helping children feel relatively secure in the short term and face the immediate tasks of growing up, we need to take a step back and look at the types of skills children need over the long term to deal with situations that they have never confronted in their lives. We must all live with the uncertainty that is part of life and the likelihood of frightening events in the future. Most important, we need to help children become the type of adults who can contribute to a better future for life on earth.

This is a tall order. It requires a number of personality characteristics that most of us value but often allow to take a back seat in the stresses of everyday life. For example, successfully facing new dangers requires the abilities to form relationships, to seek out others one can trust in times of stress, and to be able to express one's feelings in these relationships and solve problems together. This would seem like an obvious and self-evident characteristic, yet in recent years, due to the demands of work and our desire to have our children in formal educational or caretaking settings for longer and longer hours, relationships have taken a back seat. The abilities to trust, seek out others, and work in small groups can't be developed without mothers and fathers spending many hours a day with their children, nurturing closeness and intimacy, exploring and accepting feelings, and setting examples of patience, tolerance, and cooperation.

Chapter One defines short-term strategies to help in difficult times. Chapter Two describes the characteristics of a secure child who can cope with an uncertain world; this chapter also sets out long-term goals we need to set for our children in order for them to be secure and prepare for a better future.

In spite of our best efforts, however, parents should expect to see signs of stress and distress as children grow. The key is to turn anxiety or distress, or the emergence of symptoms, into opportunities for growth. A sign of distress reveals not just that particular concern, but also an area of a child's personality that needs further emphasis or work. Chapters Three, Four, and Five look closely at infants and preschoolers, school-age children, and adolescents to see what developmental tasks they need to master to be secure. We will then look at the most common signs of stress and distress, and the most frequent symptoms children have at each of these ages that suggest that they are not handling stress as effectively as possible. These symptoms are windows of opportunity for further growth that show ways to help children master their fears and face problems with increasing maturity.

The concluding chapter discusses why helping children feel more secure is so important at this time. Our children live in a more interdependent world than we have known in the past. As we are learning, we find that there won't be any barriers between ourselves and other groups. All groups will increasingly find themselves together in the same lifeboat. The ability to understand and work with others, to find collaborative solutions to conflicts, will be of growing importance.

Children cannot be truly secure in isolation. They must be part of a secure set of relationships not only in their families but in our communities and our nations. True security will be found only in secure societies. In an interdependent world, this will occur when all children and their families feel they have opportunities to meet their basic needs and pursue full and rewarding lives.

# 1

.......

# Four Basic Principles to Help Children Feel Secure during Uncertain Times

WHAT ARE THE EFFECTS OF LARGE-SCALE TRAGEDIES such as terrorist attacks, school shootings, or natural disasters on babies, children, and their families? In our roles as parents, we have to address such old and new issues as our children grow up. Today, because of a new awareness that our safety, our economy, and our environment are global issues, families have had to face a new sense of uncertainty. We are in this together.

The interdependency of disparate societies has been gradually developing over many years. Apart from the links created by modern communication through the Internet and global TV, such as CNN, the volatility of interconnected world financial markets can affect the livelihood of individual families. Shared dangers, such as global warming, pollution, and, more recently, increased terrorism, are making all of us feel very insecure.

For the last couple of years, a number of military leaders have been talking and writing about their expectation that there would be some sort of terrorist action against the United States in the near future, but none of us wanted to pay attention to their warnings. These warnings materialized into fact, shocking us into the reality that we're all tied to one another. We need not wait for other warnings—political or environmental—to come true in order to realize that we will either survive or falter as a planet—as a whole.

No walls are high enough to protect one country from another. Because relatively small groups can now threaten the entire world, we must move to another level in the way we relate to one another. The interdependency we have through communications and economies has a constructive side. If international relations remain conflictual, however, the destructive interdependency increases.

While all adults need to take leadership roles over the long run to support enlightened policies for communities and nations, the task for parents is an immediate and urgent one. We need to help our children cope with the frightening feelings that the media coverage of disasters and the anxieties of adults bring up.

There are a number of specific experiences that can help individual children and families feel more secure. Before looking into the nature of these experiences at particular ages, I'd like to define the four principles that underlie all of the more specific efforts that parents can make.


## The Four Principles

### Spend Time Together as a Family

The first level of security comes from time spent together as a whole family. In other words, the first level of security comes from being with the people you trust in an intimate relationship. It also means having enough time with that person to feel that the everyday world you live in is a reliable and safe one in which you feel protected. That can come only from warm, nurturing relationships.

The hustle-bustle of daily life needs to take a secondary position to the importance of protective and soothing relationships within the family. Family relationships are especially essential for our infants, preschoolers, and school-age children, but also for teenagers and young adults. It's equally important for mothers and fathers and other family members, because they too feel more security when they are together.

## Expressing Feelings

Next, parents need to help children express their feelings and concerns. This means giving them the time, empathy, and support to do so. Quick, hurried reassurance does not allow children to get all their feelings out. It's very, very difficult to hear a frightened child talk about his fear that somebody close to him will be killed or that he will himself be killed and to hear him ask questions like, "Can this happen to us?" Parents first need to listen. Reassurance has its role a few minutes after the child has a chance to explain his fears.

Parents can listen, empathize, and help children share what's on their minds in play as well as in verbal exchanges. As children are getting it all out, we can help them by summarizing or paraphrasing what they are saying, asking them if this is what they are feeling and trying to help them articulate it. Parents and other caregivers need to be good listeners, good empathizers, and good collaborators to help children express their concerns. For all of us, it's reassuring to know you are being listened to and that someone can hear you.

## Reassurance

The third step that can help children feel secure is to begin offering some reassurance. However, the reassurance should be couched in realistic terms. In other words, children will want to know what you are doing for them as a mommy, as a daddy, or as a teacher in order to make sure that they're protected. Here, it's important to go through the steps you are taking to make sure that children are protected and safe in their home, just as it is important to go through the steps that the government is taking. For example, children need to know that they will be seeing more people at airports or train stations who are checking tickets and bags; that there will be more guards or police to make sure that the wrong people don't get into big buildings, or schools, or onto planes. These explanations will keep children from being shocked, surprised, or confused by what changes they see. These explanations must be pitched to the level that the child can understand. Obviously, with a four-year-old you might not go into the same detail as you might for a fourteen-year-old. For a four-year-old, you might just say that mommy and daddy and others are all going to be taking care of him and making sure that he is safe, and that there will be extra people to watch and make sure that no bad people get near him or anyone else. Each age group will have its own set of concerns, and we will go into that in later chapters.

### Contributions and Helping Others

Finally, children, as well as adults, benefit from the ability to contribute something to others in need and to help in some way. Many educators are working with children in classrooms around raising funds for victims of disasters or designing projects that can help with public health or safety. From recycling to bake sales to writing letters to "adopting" public spaces, both the tiny efforts and the grander ones can make children feel more secure and not helpless. When children (and adults) have a sense of being directly involved and doing something positive and constructive to help a problem, everyone gains both energy and confidence.

These four principles play themselves out in special ways in children at different ages and in children with special needs, such as learning and developmental problems. It's often hard to figure out how much children grasp of the events of the day. How much should we talk to them about what's going on?

A good rule of thumb is to assume that such children will understand things at their appropriate levels of functional language development—not their reading, math, or test-taking levels, but in terms of their ability to carry on verbal exchanges, in other words, the level at which they can engage in an ordinary conversation. If a child can say, "Gee, I want to go outside" and we say, "Why, Susie?" and Susie says, "Because I want to play," that child has a level of causal thinking that allows her to understand the answer to a "why" question. Such a child will want to know the reason someone attacked America. At a slightly older age, children may ask if it is going to happen again. They have the beginnings of logical thinking.

Let's walk through some of the differences at some of the developmental ages (not always the same as chronological ages) so that you can see guideposts for reassuring children at each age.

## A Developing Sense of Security

### Babies and Toddlers

Babies and toddlers will sense the atmosphere in the home and in other settings, for example, day-care centers. For that reason, it is important for the adults in their lives to provide extra nurturing care at home and elsewhere. Babies can sense anxiety. Toddlers will see fleeting images on TV and will hear things that are scary. We have to monitor their access to TV and pictures that they might see in newspapers or magazines.

### Preschoolers

For preschoolers who are partially verbal but not yet logical, it is pretty much the same as for babies and toddlers, only here we use a lot of play. Pretend play, which can use many words and gestures together, is great at this age. Parents and others can get down on the floor with the children and let them play out their concerns. Parents can play back a theme to show that they understand what their children are saying (giving words to what they are playing or doing). If a child is knocking things down, a parent can say, "Oh boy. Scary stuff happening", and then ask out loud how they can make things better. It's a good idea to give words to preschoolers' actions, because while they are only beginning to get more verbal, they will often understand more than they can express. This is also true for children with special needs who are at the level of fragmented, precausal thinking.

### Early School-Age Children

Early school-age children, kindergarteners, and first- and second-graders are capable of logical thinking. They can be scared by what they see on TV (if they watch any TV) and they, too, should be protected from viewing shows or news broadcasts that are likely to be too realistic about the events of the day. Children will pick up pieces of what's going on and may worry about things happening to them, to family members, and to friends. The steps I mentioned before all need to be employed, from providing more nurturing care to helping them express their feelings, telling them how they will be protected, and getting them involved in projects to help others.

For seven- to ten- and eleven-year-olds, providing feelings of security is a special challenge. Children of these ages are very aware of what's going on but still tend to be all-or-nothing thinkers. They get stuck in fixed beliefs. Some of the more anxious seven- to ten-year-olds will get very worried and have nightmares and fears. They won't be easily reassured that nothing will happen to them or to someone they care about. They will develop their own theories about why an event has happened, and these will often be inaccurate. Nonetheless, children of this age will cling to these theories in a very intense way. Because of this, simply going through the four steps we mentioned before may not be reassuring enough.

For those children we have to provide a very soothing, nurturing atmosphere over the long haul. Children between ages seven and ten know some facts of current events but don't have the ability to put these into perspective. They have the words without the coping capacities. At this age, children are typically just learning how to recognize gray areas in an issue or multiple causes of events. If something is scary, it's hard for them to figure out if it's very scary, medium scary, a little bit scary, or just a tiny, tiny little bit scary. So, every fear can feel like a huge fear. We need to help them with gray-area thinking. For example, if something happened in another state, does that mean it's definitely going to happen here? It may, but it probably won't. We have to take it very slowly and help them reason it through. We have to help them look at more than one cause for an event. If they fasten onto one reason for causality, we need to help them look at other reasons. This can help them with a developmental milestone they would need to confront in any case.

### Teenagers

Teenagers—children who are going through puberty and the teenage years—also need all four kinds of parental attention we mentioned before, but they also need reassurance that there is going to be a future. Beyond soothing, nurturing care, more time together as a family, talking about their feelings, and considering the probability that things will or won't happen, teenagers need to participate with us in thinking about how to create a better future, a long-term plan. Such opportunities give teenagers and young adults a focus to help them deal with some of the anxieties of the moment and become the type of adults needed for the future.

## Children with Special Needs

In general, children with special needs will also sense the anxiety in the atmosphere and can become very frightened because they may not be able to ask questions or understand explanations well about the changed mood or scary images.

For these children, it is important to provide security through our presence. These children will experience security through knowing that there is an adult available who can nurture them, take care of them, and create soothing experiences. Also, they will benefit from opportunities to play out the images they may see that scare them. Children may play out themes of violence, such as dolls falling down or towers of blocks collapsing more than ever before. By providing some extra soothing and empathizing with them using simple words, such as "Things are falling. It's kind of scary, isn't it?" the parents can soothe their less verbal children and show them how to build the blocks back up again. This can be very reassuring.

A wise assumption to make for all children, but especially for children with special needs, is that they are taking in more than you think they are. Sometimes, children can understand far more than they can express in conversation. Also, you can assume that some of what children with communication difficulties take in is confused or fragmented because of the way they process information. For that reason, there is the possibility that they are a little more scared than you might assume.

The four steps we have mentioned—family time together, helping children express themselves through play and conversation, reassurance, and contributing to and helping others—are all critically important for children with special needs. Therefore, in working with children with special needs and developmental problems, we use the same principles we use with children of other ages—but you need to adapt the principles to the age level of the child's thinking. For example, for a child who is six years old but who thinks like a three-year-old, we would employ the same principles that we would with a three-year-old.

## The Larger Picture

No matter how much we reassure our children, their sense of security will depend a great deal on how we as parents view the world. We have to be aware that all children, even babies and preschoolers, will sense our own anxiety. They will sense any tension at home, in the classroom, and in community meeting places where people are discussing tragic events (even if they're not hearing the content or the words directly). Older children—from nine- to ten-year-olds to teenagers—will ask us many hard questions about the issues involved.

In order for parents to be able to reassure their children and teenagers, they have to assess their own feelings about the future. One teenager asked me the other day, "How do we know that there won't be more attacks? What if there are even worse weapons, like biological and chemical or nuclear? How do we know that won't happen?" I said, "Honestly, we don't. But what we need to do is to reduce the long-term likelihood of that. What I hope our government will do is advocate long-term policies that make such attacks less likely." I explained that I meant reducing, over time, the number of people who want to give up their lives to destroy other people. Each family will have to think out its own view of the future and how it can be made more secure.

Until children and families in every part of the world have certain basics—adequate food and housing and protection; opportunities for nurturing childcare in stable families and stable communities; and  opportunities for education, especially an education characterized by an appreciation of different perspectives around the globe, the likelihood of destructive conflict will continue. As part of a program for the future, we need to make sure that in addition to having these basic needs met, there are opportunities for economic and personal growth so that all people have something to look forward to. This will require greater understanding and tolerance for different goals and cultural aspirations of different peoples around the world.

If we really want children to feel secure in the future, we have to help people elsewhere feel secure. It will not be easy, because it means being concerned about a child with AIDS in Africa as well as children in our own neighborhood or family. To extend our empathy in this way is a new developmental milestone for all of us. However, in an interdependent world our own "backyard" has no boundaries. It is literally the globe. As I expressed to my teenage friend, I hope that, while we all have to take immediate actions to improve security at local and national levels, we also need to have much more forward-looking plans that will address the root causes of terrorism, epidemics, and pollution. Such threats may always be with us, but if we can support long-term international planning, rather than reactive and repressive measures, the severity of these problems can be reduced.

Such long-term concerns may seem far removed from the immediacy of a child's feelings of security. However, as adults we must be concerned about the future of children to come. Unless we are involved in shaping this future, we may ourselves convey an attitude of uncertainty and anxiety to our families. Because much violence and instability come from huge discrepancies between the ability of different groups to provide the basics of life, the most powerful groups will be viewed with anger and suspicion. To reduce the rage, the economically better-off groups need to understand more clearly and deal with the needs of those with whom we share the globe. Because we cannot wall ourselves off from infectious diseases, pollution, or terrorist attacks within our own country, let alone from without, true security will come only from recognizing interdependence, from programs of human capital investment, and from full cooperation in international treaties and organizations. These three goals must be vigorously pursued.

Our teenagers and older children won't be satisfied—and most of us won't feel secure—unless we know that there are intelligent long-term plans in place that build security for the future. We need not only to deal with immediate anxieties in the ways I will outline here, but also to become involved, in whatever way our abilities and resources allow, in educational, political, economic, or scientific efforts to reduce known threats to later generations.

# 2

# What Makes a Secure Child?

WHEN WE THINK ABOUT WHAT MAKES A CHILD SECURE, IT'S IMPOR-tant to realize that we're talking about what happens both within the child's consciousness and within her family. As a child is growing, developing, and forming her personality, she's grad-ually learning to feel more secure or insecure. Her inner state is heavily influenced by ongoing relationships with parents, sib-lings, and others. It's difficult, if not impossible, for a child to feel secure in a family that's not providing the kind of nurturing support and empathy the child requires. Even a seemingly in-dependent child who is a good student and has lots of friends may be quite insecure on a deeper level if she feels she can't rely on her mom and/or dad. Similarly, a child who may appear inse-cure, for example, anxiously coming into her parents' bedroom at night and otherwise seeking them out all the time, may feel secure deep down if she knows she can count on her parents to be there when she needs them. She may feel free to express her need for them because she knows that they will respond.

## Family Relationships

This point was illustrated for me recently when I was helping parents with two very different types of children. The first was four-year-old Teddy, a preschooler who had been allowed to see many images of war and violence on TV and who would play out scenes of devastation such as tanks knocking buildings down, hurricanes, or gun battles. Generally, all the doll figures got severely injured in these pretend tragedies. When he played on his own, the scenes tended to repeat themselves. In fact, it was for this reason, as well as for a kind of unreachable and anxious quality in his behavior, that his parents sought consultation, wondering what they could do to help him cope with the obvious concerns being expressed in his play.

It hadn't occurred to Teddy's parents to get down on the floor and become a partner in his dramas so that he could work out his concerns as part of a relationship. In fact, when I suggested that to his father in my office, he looked somewhat alarmed. It turned out that this father had two older brothers and was initiated into the rough-and-tumble world at a very early age. He learned to protect himself from being picked on and took part in various types of sports. As a result, he did very little imaginative play as a child. He also described his parents as very busy, matter-of-fact people.

With a little encouragement, however, the father relaxed, got down on the floor, and started joining Teddy's play. Initially, I didn't do much coaching. When Teddy made his airplanes or cars crash, however, just his dad's presence led to an interesting change. Teddy was telling his dad what to do. "Crash this car and this truck." Dad was dutifully obeying. Then with a little encouragement from me, in addition to playing out the role that Teddy had assigned him, occasionally Dad would amplify and say, "Boy, I have a powerful truck here! I'm really going to knock these guys over!" At other times, with my encouragement, Dad would just make a summary comment such as, "Wow, there are a lot of people getting knocked over here!"

After about fifteen minutes of this joint play, a very interesting change occurred. Instead of each drama ending in chaos, with everything knocked over, Teddy began finding solutions.

For example, ambulances came in to help the injured. As the father continued playing with Teddy at home, slowly but surely Teddy brought in police to control and limit the bad dolls from knocking over the good ones. Over a period of time—less than three weeks—Teddy began shifting from purely aggressive themes to play that was associated with solutions. Teddy himself seemed more relaxed as his play themes broadened beyond just aggression. At home, there was a recurrence of his "old warmth," as his parents described it. He had a brighter look in his eyes, they said. In addition, he sought them out for more cuddles, hugs, and comfort.

In this particular example, for Teddy a sense of security required active efforts from his family. His ability to weather the images he had seen on TV depended on his parents' joining him with their warm, nurturing presence. When this was made available, he showed lots of the characteristics (we will describe them later) of being a secure child, with a flexible imagination and initiative in finding solutions. On his own, however, this same child was showing behavior characteristic of a more insecure child, repeating scary games but with no variety or solutions. For Teddy, the renewed relationship with his father made all the difference.

My encounter with Sally, an eight-year-old girl, also illustrated the importance of family relationships. She was coming home from school very worried about her dad, who worked in downtown Washington, D.C. She worried about his getting "germs" or about "bad people" hurting him. She would anxiously pace around the kitchen, stating her fears. Sally was an organized, thoughtful little girl who was very sensitive to everything going on around her. She was a neat child, even to the point of lining up her shoes the night before so she could get dressed quickly in the morning. She was a A-student who did her homework on time and was generally obedient and responsive to her parents' wishes. She had a number of close, warm friendships and was very considerate. She didn't miss a trick. In many respects, her parents considered her a model child and quite secure because she was doing so well in so many areas. She seemed at home in this busy family where Dad worked full-time and Mom worked part-time, often, however, doing extra work at home.

It turned out that when Sally came home from school worried about her father, her mother would often be finishing up some work she'd brought home from the office. Mother kept trying to encourage Sally to go out and play with her friends (who lived close by). Mother also encouraged her to "take your mind off of it. Do your homework instead." Most of her suggestions were ways of gently saying, "Can't you see I'm busy? We'll talk when Daddy comes home later. I need to finish up my work."

You can already guess what my first idea was. I suggested that when Sally came home, her mother should spend the first half-hour or hour being very available to her, talking about or playing out whatever concerned her. Mother could catch up on her work in the evening when the father came home. Somewhat reluctantly, she agreed to try out this idea. Like her daughter, she was very organized and liked to get things done in a certain sequence. She wanted to be done with her work before it was time to make dinner. Nonetheless, the mother agreed to the new approach for at least three or four weeks to see if it would make a difference.

Now, when Sally came home, Mom would be "all ears," hanging on Sally's every word. She empathized with her worries, learning about whether or not other children were worried about their daddies, and so forth. Mom also learned about the subtle nuances of Sally's feelings—whether she felt more worried today than yesterday. She went into a little more depth about what Sally thought might happen to her daddy if he were exposed to "bad germs." As Mom empathized and listened, she was surprised at the level of detail she heard from her daughter. Sally remembered her grandfather's death only a few years ago.

She had vivid images of him in his last months looking very weak and remembered how scary it was when he couldn't talk to her very clearly as he got much weaker. She also talked about how much she missed her grandfather, who had lived not far away, and how he used to come over and play with her when she was younger.

Her mother was also surprised to hear how "mad" Sally was at the bad people who were hurting other people. She wanted to have them locked up in jail so they couldn't hurt anyone anymore. Sally, who was very articulate about her feelings, could go on for hours and hours, much like an adult who loves to talk. However, her mother found that if she made herself available for about forty to sixty minutes or so initially and stayed very calm and empathetic, Sally seemed to share what was on her mind and then set out on her own to play with her friends.

The mother was also greatly interested in the fact that even though Sally was talking about scary feelings, by the fourth or fifth day of such talks Sally's emotions had changed somewhat. Rather than talking in an agitated way, repeating many of her fears over and over, Sally seemed to enjoy having the person she probably loved the most in the world listening to her. There was growing softness and pleasure in little phrases like, "Well, let me tell you more about this!" The joy of being heard and listened to and the security that it offered helped Sally experience some new emotions of comfort, security, and well-being, even though she was talking about frightening events. As Sally talked and her mother empathized with her, her mother could see the comfort come across Sally's face. As time went on, Sally gradually seemed to need only about thirty to thirty-five minutes of the mother's undivided time when she came home from school before wanting to run out and play with her friends.

As you can see from these two examples, while children can display secure or insecure behavior, security is a state of being or feeling that resides both in the child and in the relationships the child has with her mother, father, and, often, siblings or extended family. This also can include relationships with teachers and others who are important to the child. For young children in day care, it may involve day-care staff as well. Therefore, we need to look at the kind of relationships throughout childhood that support or don't support a sense of security. We also need to look at the characteristics of children that show they are, in fact, developing a sense of security, such as an interest in sharing feelings and mastering age-expected problems.

## Resilience

In discussing the characteristics of a secure child, it is important to touch upon the concept of resilience. Resilience and security have a lot in common. Some colleagues and many parents think of resilience as the ability to be tough in the face of stress, to have a thick skin, to be able to bounce back. To be sure, everyone would like to be able to bounce back and not be too overwhelmed by stress, but this is a superficial and incomplete notion of resilience. A thick-skinned child who doesn't show signs of being upset when stressed and who seems to try to take charge of situations, be a leader, and be assertive may or may not be truly assertive. Alternatively, a child who's undergone lots of stress in his or her life, including poverty and many family problems, yet nonetheless succeeds academically, in a career, or in family life may certainly show a component of resilience, but true resilience means much more.

What is really meant by resilience here is the ability to enter fully into life's opportunities and meet its challenges without compromising any essential aspects of our humanity. So, for example, a child who bounces back from adversity but isn't able to empathize or understand others is not fully resilient. Such a child is likely to have a limited quality of life and a lack of intimacy as an adult with a spouse or children. Children who haven't learned to empathize with others will have paid a big price for their earlier adversity. They will have coped as well as they could under the circumstances, and while we applaud what they did accomplish, we would not apply the term resilient.

When resilient individuals experience adversity, they are somehow able to retain a full range of feelings and abilities. They are not just assertive but can tolerate within themselves and their relationships a wide range of feelings, from fear, anxiety, and sadness to joy, confidence, and mastery. At times, they can be overwhelmed or sad, anxious or worried. This is part of their human drama, and they put that into context in order to better solve the next group of challenges they have. In other words, they don't get lost in their sad, worried, or anxious feelings of the moment; they use the experience to find solutions. Resilient people don't appear competent or even strong all the time. Like all of us, they seemingly vacillate between moments of strength and weakness. However, beneath these moments lies the genuine resilience that allows a person to grow and use the sorrows or frustrations to become a fuller, deeper, and more humane person in the future.

Just as we think of the secure child as one who grows within relationships in his or her family that promote security, so too the resilient child is part of resilient relationships. In other words, resiliency is not an attribute of the child alone, but reflects her relationships. For example, the best known and most complete study of resilience was of children growing up on an island off of Hawaii. These children were exposed to poverty and lots of family problems early in life. The authors of the study found that certain of these children survived the adversities and did reasonably well as they got older. It was discovered that these children had a hidden strength that seemed to be an important component of their ability to rise above their troubles. This hidden strength was not physical or intellectual strength. Rather, the strength was in having access to a nurturing relationship with a relative or someone else, a person who lived across the way in another house or across the hall in a building.

Having a relationship that was consistently nurturing and sup-portive was an important factor in separating the resilient chil-dren from the less resilient children. In the study, resilience was shown to be not a state of mind, but rather the state of the relationships the child had available. No child can grow and de-velop in an emotionally healthy way without nurturing relation-ships.

Some children require different relationship patterns than others, and sometimes luck is involved in the kinds of relation-ships the child has available. A child who is very self-absorbed will get lost in a chaotic family where there's not a great deal of support. In that family, a child who's eager, reaches out, and makes a lot of noise may turn out to be the resilient one be-cause she will get more nurturing interaction and care, which may be very limited in that family to begin with.

Another study done in poor Mexican villages found that mothers favored (gave more breast-feeding time and breast milk) to their physically more needy babies (babies with low muscle tone or those who couldn't suck well). Babies who showed physical characteristics early on that are ordinarily as-sociated with vulnerability got more of mother's nurturing care and interaction because of the natural maternal instincts of car-ing for the weak and helpless. In the Mexican villages, these children fared better in their development because they re-ceived more nurturing care, even though they were, in some respects, physically more vulnerable. They—not their physi-cally more adept counterparts—ended up being the more re-silient ones.

Therefore, we can consider resilience in the same way as we do a sense of security, as a product of the relationships the child has with her caregivers and how well these relationships can meet the child's unique developmental profile. It's this larger context that determines how resilient a child will be. The child's physical makeup is one component, but relationships that either meet or don't meet the child's needs will determine overall resilience. Simply looking at poverty and children who survive poverty, or looking at disruptive families and children who survive in those settings, doesn't reveal the essence of resiliency. That comes from a closer understanding of the nature of the particular relationships children have in these different settings. A resilient child is, therefore, a secure child.

## Characteristics of a Secure Child

The main characteristics and relationship patterns that define a secure child are laid out here along with signs or worrisome patterns that reveal insecurities. No child or adult has all these characteristics, but most have some of them, more or less.

### The Ability to Engage In and Rely On Vital Relationships with Mother, Father, and Siblings, As Well As Other Adults

This is probably the most important attribute of the secure child: having enough trust in relationships so that he or she can use them in times of stress to feel better and find solutions. It's easy to take this attribute for granted. Most of us have family relationships and relationships at work and/or at school. As we look at our children, and children in general, we see very different patterns, however. We see children who, when they're upset, haul themselves off to their rooms to play alone. Others escape into fantasy, babbling to themselves about what's worrying them but in an isolated, repetitive way. Other children escape into computers or TV watching. Some children expect relationships to lead to fights. They may seek out relationships but do so provocatively through fighting or by getting their parents irritated all the time. As my distinguished colleague Reginald Lourie once said, "These are children who seek out love through irritation."

The capacity for using relationships begins early in life with four-month-olds wooing their parents into smiling at them by smiling every time the parent walks by. With an eight-month-old, this occurs as the child flirts more dramatically with give-and-take smiles and peek-a-boo games. It's present in a three-and-a-half-year-old who comes into Mom's bed when there's a scary thunderstorm or he's had bad dream and is able to ask for comforting. It occurs in an eight-year-old who's able to complain to mommy and daddy about school and the mean teacher, rather than keeping it all locked up inside. All of these examples show a child using relationships, trusting relationships, and finding them reassuring.

Relationships don't exist simply for the purpose of relieving stress, however. They have to be a part of the child's everyday life, with family members, friends, and others sharing pleasures, joys, and anger, in order for the child to trust and use them when problems arise. Children who have the ability to use relationships like to be with their parents and "friendly" siblings, as well as other warm, nurturing, empathetic adults most of the time. These children also show the ability to discriminate. They may avoid an adult who's too aggressive or bossy. Even quite a small child will size up someone who is very controlling and hide in her mother's legs or exit into another room.

## The Ability to Communicate a Full Range of Feelings and Desires

When we think about a child's ability to communicate, we usually think of how she uses words or pretend play. But we all have a more basic level of communication. This is the ability to show, without words, how we are feeling—looking happy and joyful, looking upset, getting ready for being negative or stubborn, mobilizing for some anger. All these expressions of feeling involve different body postures, facial expressions, and arm and leg gestures.

Such gestures allow others to understand how someone is feeling. But they also enable each one of us to comprehend how we feel. As we tighten our faces in an angry glare, that helps us know we're feeling angry. The gesture helps us feel it. When we brighten up, have a gleam in our eyes, and a big smile on our face, it supports the feeling of happiness.

We don't feel happy and then make our faces smile and show delight. It happens as one smooth process. There's lots of evidence to suggest that the feeling tone in our bodies helps us appreciate in ourselves how we're feeling. In other words, expressing feelings is both a physical and a mental process. This doesn't mean when you are feeling sad and you fake a smile you will feel happy. The mental and physical aspects of feelings work together. The physical expression supports and deepens the mental process. There are also infinite variations on how feelings are expressed physically. It's kind of a personal signature.

Now why is this so important in feeling secure? Many of us can't communicate as quickly with words as we can with our gestures. A smile or an unhappy or puzzled look happens very quickly. In relationships, an empathetic partner (whether it's a spouse, a a good friend, or a parent to a child) responds quickly, even before the words get communicated. That person responds with a gesture of his or her own. If we're looking angry, a good friend will look concerned and want to give us a look of "tell me about it." If we're delighted, a good friend will brighten up with a smile, sharing our joy and making our joy even deeper. Imagine how you feel when you're delighted with something you've just done (you've come up with a great idea or done some other feat worthy of great pleasure, or perhaps you just heard your child say her first word) and you beam with delight. If your partner looks critical or annoyed at you, it ruins the fun. The joy is drained right out of your body as though you've done something wrong. In other words, these rapid exchanges of expression are the first line of communication, far quicker than words and far more important, in many respects, than words.

If a child is unable to express her feelings through gestures and is unable to show joy, sorrow, curiosity, annoyance, or frustration, we can't respond back in this affirming way, and we can't help the child elaborate. If a child looks annoyed and we give her a soft, understanding look of "What's the matter?" we encourage her to show us what's the matter. She may then take us to a toy she can't fix or to the refrigerator. Children often do this even before they're two years old. Even eight- and nine-year-olds will respond positively to a warm, soft look that encourages them to show what's upsetting them.

Children who are unable to express their emotions through facial expression, body posture, and/or other gestures are often prone to being aggressive. Beginning in the preschool years but going into the school years, they seem unable to show their annoyance before they act out impulsively. In other words, they go from a standing start to full steam ahead in a split second. Rather than grimacing, showing annoyance, warning with facial expressions, and so on, that they're about to have a fit, they just act it out. Children who can warn with their facial expressions and who have responsive caregivers, generally tend to get either a limit-setting or reassuring look back. Let's say the child shows a look that suggests she's about to push a peer or sibling. The tuned-in mom or dad will look back at her with a stern expression and maybe a hand held palm out, like the corner policeman, and that helps the child settle down. When a child is worried or scared, an understanding look sometimes will help the child feel a little more secure.

The parents of children who are aggressive without showing signs of an impending outburst tend to be preoccupied and not naturally skilled at responding to their child's gestures. This isn't true in every case of an impulsive child. There are many different family dynamics. But when the child lacks the ability to show how she is feeling ahead of time, the tendency to act out quickly can be intensified by parents who do not read their children's emotional expressions well, or are themselves emotionally unexpressive.

This system of communication through facial expressions and gestures develops initially in infancy and reaches a high point in the second year of life when toddlers are using their gestures to communicate before they have words. It continues throughout the school, adolescent, and adult years. It's a system that continues to develop in parallel along with our words. It's a faster system—it's the one we trust more, and the one we rely on more. I like to use the example of an adult being on a dark street in the city. A menacing looking stranger comes up and asks the time. Do you act on the menacing look and move away, or do you trust the harmless words and linger to give him the time?

This system, which we use to negotiate safety, danger, fear, acceptance, approval, and so on, is absolutely essential for feeling secure. Without having this ability to express one's own feelings and read and respond to other people's feelings swiftly as part of two-way communication, one feels very unsure in a busy, confusing world where too much is happening too quickly to be processed verbally.

This same ability also helps children negotiate peer relationships, to understand and read other children's feelings. A child who goes to school and doesn't sense when other children want to play with her or not may move in too closely to other children, crowding them, putting her nose too close to the other child's face. When the other child starts shifting away, she persists and the other child just gets more irritated with her. Children said to have poor "social" skills often actually have problems in reading and responding to gestural communication. Such a child will often end up feeling hurt, confused, and insecure.

As an example of this, I remember a child who, when he felt happy, would simply run over and hug the other children. He was eight years old and wasn't able to anticipate who wanted to be hugged or didn't want to be hugged and he didn't have other ways to share his joy and happiness, such as just giggling together. Just like the child who doesn't signal when he's feeling aggressive but instead just acts out impulsively, this child didn't know how to express his own happiness in any way other than immediate action. He had never seemed to develop beyond the level of the eight- and nine-month-old who reaches up his hands, gives a beautiful smile and a big hug. This is what we hope for in a child of that age, but not one older than that.

There appeared to be two reasons for this child's problem. One was that he had little opportunity for play. Both parents were working, and this child grew up with a nanny that the parents think, in retrospect, was somewhat self-absorbed and a little depressed. While this person could guarantee physical safety, she wasn't doing a lot of interacting. The nanny cared for him during that period of about twelve to twenty-eight months, when this system of communication would have been developed. Also, when the parents were home in the evenings, they admitted reluctantly, they had been very preoccupied and work oriented. The only way this little boy got their attention was through frontal assaults—jumping in and giving big hugs and kisses. In this particular family there hadn't been an opportunity for learning this sensitive emotional signaling.

We often see this type of behavior in children who have some processing difficulties and visual/spatial-processing problems. Such children don't find it as easy as other children to figure out a facial expression because their ability to comprehend what they see takes them a little longer.

In times of great stress or loss this ability for expressing feelings takes on greater importance. It enables a child to communicate how she is feeling even if she hasn't the words to express it. Many children haven't the words to express confusion, bewilderment, anxiety, and concern, but parents can see it in their eyes, facial expressions, and body posture. A child who's worried but is saying, "I'm fine," may be communicating otherwise through her facial expressions and body posture. The child may have sad expressions and may mope around a bit more before she herself recognizes how she is feeling.

At the preschool level, children are just learning how to express verbally how they're feeling and can't yet do so for complicated feelings like sadness, worry, or anxiety. They can't yet find the words for these. Therefore, gesturing is a primary way for parents to understand and comfort their children at times of stress and confusion.

Similarly, grade-school children are often not yet able to express some complicated feelings. Even if they have the ability to express their emotions, they may choose not to because it's "scary." However, they can show the emotion in their facial expressions and gestures. This allows the parent to begin responding with their own gestures (looking concerned, empathetic, or warm, or setting limits, where needed). As mentioned earlier, there's nothing more reassuring to a child, or an adult for that matter, than to have a partner, caregiver, close friend, or spouse who, through his or her own emotional responses, demonstrates to you at a deep personal level that you're being understood. The look in the parents' eyes as they read their child's look correctly is the first and most important aspect of helping that child feel more secure. That's why in such situations we work with children on learning this basic skill through floor time and other strategies described in Chapter Three. This skill can't be taught by lecturing or practicing rote drills, like taking turns or using polite phrases.

It's also important to emphasize that the ability to express feelings and respond to them with gestures needs to be learned for all the feelings that are part of our humanity—not just love and happiness, but also assertiveness and anger, loss, fear, humiliation, and so forth. A secure child can experience, express, and comprehend the full human range.

### The Ability to Solve Problems and Take Initiative

Early in life, often before two years of age, we learn to solve problems, to change situations that are upsetting us. Later, this involves verbal problem-solving and gets developed further all the way until we're adults. An eight-month-old initiates games with mommy and daddy, reaches for the rattle, and engages you in a peek-a-boo game. By fourteen to fifteen months, toddlers are seeking you out, bringing you a toy or a book, pointing to what they want, and dragging you places to help them in what they want to do. Without this ability, toddlers feel helpless, withdraw, or just cry when they want something.

You can easily understand that a child who has developed the ability to figure how to get what she wants will feel more secure about the world. A preschooler who's feeling scared and is able to come and get you to give her a long cuddle ("not a little one—a big, big, big one") will feel the world is a safer place. In contrast, the more helpless and passive preschooler may just get upset and be finicky and irritable and you'll have to guess why.

Similarly, school-age children who let you know when some kids are being mean can enlist your help in finding a solution. Other children, by this age, may find solutions on their own and not need to involve you in their "playground politics."

This problem-solving orientation and attitude keeps developing through the school years and into adolescence. We can see the differences between kids, for example, in the way they get ready for a job or college. There are those who get the applications on their own and then seek out their parents, school counselors, or other adults for guidance, and there are those who feel overwhelmed or play "ostrich," and all of a sudden find themselves at the deadline for college or job applications without having done the preliminary work.

The problem-solving orientation enables children to feel a sense of security in that they can deal with the world, even when the world is challenging. When there are extreme challenges—an unsafe neighborhood, illness in families, or disaster on a large scale—a problem-solving orientation is essential. Children need to be able to seek us out when they're worried or scared. As they get older, they need to feel part of the problem-solving efforts of their families, workplaces, and society. A can-do attitude is vital in times of stress.

We will see ways to foster this attitude in the preschool, elementary school, or adolescent years in Chapters Three, Four, and Five.

The key is to provide the nurturing support from ongoing relationships that we talked about above, with a lot of interaction and negotiation, and, within those interactions, to challenge the children to be assertive. Let the baby crawl to you and reach out with her hands to be picked up, by looking at her and by putting your hands up and saying, "Come, come, come! You've got to come over here to get picked up!" For the fifteenth-month-old who's looking for that toy, play dumb so that she has to take you to three or four different places, flexing her assertive muscles, before she gets her toy. With a preschooler who says something as simple as "I want to go outside," and we say "yes" or "no," we're not inspiring assertiveness. When we ask them "why" and what they want to do, and we then say, "That's a great idea," they're getting the assurance that they can assert their ideas and that they can have good ideas. With a grade-school child, whether it's a math problem or an English problem, you might show her once how to do it, but then let her show you the way she thinks it could be done or brainstorm with her, let her come up with different possibilities, and decide which possibilities work best, but don't do it for her. In other words, challenge her to be an assertive thinker.

To do that, you have to be engaged in the relationship with children, have a lot of time for interacting with them, but not actually do the work for them. With teenagers this is even trickier, because they tend not to seek us out that much to begin with, but here, too, position yourself in the teenager's life so that she can relate to you, such as by driving her places (the car is a great time for long conversations). Instead of doing everything for her, like getting her college or job applications for her, raise questions regarding what her game plan is. If you're doing this around smaller things like summer jobs, hopefully by the time she's facing bigger challenges, like getting a real job after college, she'll have that assertive, can-do attitude.

In times of great stress, when children experience fears, anxieties, worries, or angry feelings, there will be the temptation to provide the reassurance for them, versus offering an empathetic, warm, and very available relationship in which they can work out their own feelings. With the example we gave earlier in this chapter of the little girl who was worried about her father, her mother could ask, "What do you think would help with these worries?" Because there had been a lot of nurturing and discussion going on and this little girl now felt she could use her mother as an ally and a helper, she was able to explore possibilities, such as "I could call Daddy up and talk to him. That might help!" or "Actually, just talking to you a little more might help and I don't have to call Daddy." This girl could look for solutions to her anxious feelings rather than feeling overwhelmed by them.

Teenagers can be helped to become part of the policy debate on terrorism, looking at the long-term geopolitical issues and what it's going to take to increase security worldwide. They can flex their muscles and apply what they're learning in history, economics, and geography to real problems in the world. Looking to the future, even the long-term future, is an important element of being a good problem-solver.

*The Ability to Use Ideas to Express Worries As Well As a Range of Feelings*

The capacity to use ideas has been traditionally thought of as the hallmark of human functioning—separating us from nonhuman primates (our closest cousins on the evolutionary tree). It's also what separates people from other people. Some people use ideas better than others.

The ability to use ideas also contributes to a feeling of security. With ideas, children can label feelings and tell others what they're feeling—scared, worried, angry, frightened. They can discuss why they're feeling that way and can brainstorm about ways to feel better. They can explore long-term solutions to threats of danger and loss. Without the ability to use ideas, the ability to solve problems is minimal. Not all children can use ideas to the same degree, and, therefore, some children feel much more secure about the way they can shape their lives and the situations around them.

Children learn how to use ideas early in life. We see the beginnings of this with the early use of language in toddlers. By age two, we're hearing phrases and word combinations together, as well as early pretend play where the dolls are hugging or having a tea party, which is another way children express their ideas. It's important for parents to make a distinction, however, between using ideas for the purpose of conveying how a child feels or what their intentions or wishes are and using ideas simply to label things. For example, many children become quite gifted early on at identifying a couch or a chair or the zebra in the picture book. That's valuable too, but it does not contribute as much to a feeling of security as the ability to express how you feel and what you want. The child who can say, "Juice now!" is using ideas to solve a problem and get a basic need met. He's not just labeling the picture of the juice.

In the preschool years, a child who can use ideas to explain what he needs, instead of acting things out or experiencing stress, will feel more secure. In contrast, the child who gets a tummy ache or a headache instead of expressing fears is at a disadvantage.

During school-age years, a child's ability to use ideas gets developed further in all kinds of ways as she gets into more sophisticated conversations with peers and negotiations with parents. Children are able to use their ideas even when their feelings are strong—when they're very angry, sad, or feeling rejected. When they return from a rough day at school, children are able to tell their parents how upset they were. In contrast, other children may just storm into their rooms, slam the door, and turn on the TV—or beat up a sibling.

Obviously, using ideas grows in importance during the adolescent and adult years. Some adults have a wide range of ideas they can use to negotiate and express their needs and feelings, even when their feelings are strong. Others lapse into impulsive behavior or physical symptoms or become very self-involved or withdrawn. Still others throw tantrums. Ideas are the ticket to finding constructive solutions and are an essential component of a sense of security.

In helping a child feel secure in an insecure world, adults need to offer children practice in using their ideas to express a wide range of feelings. In frightening times, we all need a large vocabulary to verbalize the many different feelings that arise such as fear, anxiety, trepidation, and worry. Children worry about a great range of things. They may be frightened of losing a parent, scared of being alone in the world, or anxious about being injured themselves. They can have worries about losing control ("My brain won't work and I'll be all over the place like splattered paint"), losing their fragile sense of self, and ceasing to exist ("I'll become atomized into air"). Listening with empathy and patience can help children verbalize these scary feelings.

When families are under stress parents and educators need to help children more than ever before to use their ideas and verbalize their feelings. However, you can't just out of the blue ask a child to talk about a scary feeling unless you already have that child in a trusting and nurturing relationship with a lot of shared gestures and feelings.

### The Ability to Reason and Think

A child who can apply high levels of reasoning and thinking to her emotional and social world generally feels more secure than a child who cannot. For example, between the ages of three and five, when children are learning to build bridges between their ideas (for example, to answer "why" questions), a parent might ask, "Why are you looking worried?" The child may answer, "Because I'm worried that daddy will get hurt." The four-year-old who has learned to link ideas could give such an answer. Another four-year-old, however, might instead simply talk about the blue car outside or the red toy.

The ability to reason and think about one's emotional and social world, when applied to the emotional and social challenges of children, is complicated. Some children, for example, like to escape into fantasy when confronted with a reality-based conversation about something scary. Instead of holding onto reality, they immediately go into pretend play where they can control their world and be more magical in their thinking. Even there, these children may get a little fragmented and illogical in their thinking—from bears attacking a helpless zebra to trucks crashing a tea party. One can sense when children are having a difficult time staying with reality; they escape more into a disjointed fantasy world.

The child who can be logical and reality-based both in conversations and in pretend-play dramas has two wonderful ways to feel more secure and cope with stress, as well as to solve problems. When such a child is concerned about something, he can play it out or talk it out, and, in both cases, has a better chance to *figure it out*. In other words, if play and talk are logical and reality based, they can lead to figuring things out. If a child withdraws from reality just briefly, it is not worrisome. But it is worrisome if a child escapes into fantasy all the time. If every time a difficult subject comes up the child becomes a little more self-absorbed, retreats into make-believe, or becomes concerned with the cake she is going to have for dinner, this pattern is a sign that that child hasn't the level of thinking needed for a high level of inner security. The ability to tolerate even strong feelings while holding onto reality is one of the important characteristics of a secure child.

This ability to reason emerges during ages three to five and gets stronger during the school years, and, with expected ups and downs, it should develop more fully during the adolescent years. We expect a worried four-year-old to escape into fantasy and show some self-absorption with her own bodily needs (such as where the next ice cream is coming from) and certainly some impulsivity. But we would also expect her to be able to regroup and come back to a reality orientation when we help her, particularly when we simplify her fears so that she can understand them. For example, when a preschooler is dealing with fears of people being hurt and talking about a friend at school or her father going on an airplane and she becomes impulsive or more fragmented in her play, empathy and support should help. We might say, "I know that's kind of scary," hanging in there with her and trying to bring her back to more organized play, or we could also help her regain some logic by simply talking to her about the fact that we can tell that when she gets scared she likes to bang things sometimes and that helps her feel better. This should be enough to help the child either change the subject in a logical way ("Mommy, let's do something else now") or perhaps even elaborate a little bit more through play showing, for example, dolls being taken care of by a doctor.

During the school years, we also see a big range in the ability to be logical and reasonable. A child who says she doesn't want to talk about school or shows fears of planes crashing into the house but then doesn't want to talk about it will often give a reason. The reason might be, "I want to talk about baseball now. We've talked enough about those kinds of things." Or the child might simply say, "It doesn't bother me. It bothers you." Although the child is not dealing directly with the issue at hand, she is nonetheless staying logical and organized and showing the ability to reason. Sometimes children during the grade-school years will also escape into a world of their own or become very self-absorbed with their own needs of the moment (such as wanting more toys for Christmas). Such typical ways of coping with anxiety are ways to avoid a difficult issue. In doing this, however, they will be more likely than a preschooler to offer a bridge to a new subject—"Let's play now. Enough talk." However, when school-age children give up their hold on reality too readily and can't recover and come back to reality, that is a sign that the ability to reason that we need for inner security is not developing appropriately. If the problem continues, professional consultation may be needed.

Of course, children will vary in what they can be realistic about. Even school-age children won't be able to apply reality to the full range of topics that parents often believe they should be able to discuss. They will vary considerably in their ability to talk about illness, the death of a grandparent, scary feelings that they have, failures in school, feelings of competition and success, and even feelings of pleasure, joy, and pride. Each child can often talk about such feelings a little bit. The important thing is to keep an eye on whether the child's ability to talk about a wide range of feelings is generally moving in the right direction.

A lot depends on how the parent approaches the child. If the parent approaches a subject in a controlling way, the child will avoid any discussion. If parents engage themselves with a child through being available and through taking an interest in the child's natural interests (be it school, pretend play, or throwing a ball around), this positions the parent to be helpful. Then periodically, when parents, as part of spending time with the child, bring up some of the subjects they think the child might be thinking about and are respectful if the child doesn't want to talk about them, the odds are the child will gradually become able to talk about these subjects in a realistic and logical way.

For the "adolescent," the ability to reason about a range of subjects is much greater. However, at this age the issue of privacy is more central and the degree to which teenagers want to talk with their peers, teachers, or parents about a particular subject will vary considerably. Once again, adults need to position themselves with teenagers so that there are long periods of time during which they can talk spontaneously about the events of their lives and how they're feeling about different things. In that context, one can often bring up subjects of mutual interest. Teenagers are apt to be very explicit when they don't want to talk about things and will stay very logical even in this avoidance, often giving many reasons why parents couldn't possibly understand their complicated thoughts, and, therefore, they're not even going to bother telling them about it. Again, here, appreciate the logic of the argument, hang in, and see if over time there's a greater capacity to open up in at least some of the sensative areas for realistic discussion.

### The Ability to Grasp Multiple Causes and "Gray Areas" of Issues and Feelings

An important part of thinking that emerges during the early school years, between ages five and eight, is the ability to entertain more than one possibility. "Chris won't play with me. Is it because she hates me or just that she likes to play soccer and I like to play on the computer?" A child who can consider two or three possibilities why another child is mean to her will find life much easier than will a child who always assumes it's because the child doesn't like her ("Nobody likes me!"). Such a rigid view can become a reality when the child acts as though she has been stigmatized. The child who can see the multiple reasons for the actions of others doesn't see all the things an adult might. But at least by looking beyond the most obvious ones, she is able to find better ways to cope. When a child doesn't want to play with her, she can think, "Well, maybe it's because Chris plays soccer and I play on computers. Maybe if I practice soccer with my dad, I can go out and play soccer during recess and be friends with her too."

We know that many adults employ these tactics every day of their lives and that children who have flexible coping strategies, including indirect "roads to Rome," find many ways to meet their goals. This, in turn, gives them a greater sense of security so that they can do so in the future. When it comes to dealing with the fears caused by outside events, the child who can look at the world from multiple perspectives is better able to look at the reasons why there might be violence or conflict. For example, she might be able to see that terrorist attacks were aimed at the government or the media and, therefore, it's highly unlikely that something will happen to her home in Des Moines, Iowa. In contrast, a child who is not able to see the multiple reasons for things might assume very readily that because a gunman went berserk because he was fired, he is likely to shoot everyone else, too. Without this ability, every danger is taken personally.

The ability to see the world in terms of the multiple causes for events, particularly events that have emotional meaning, enables a child not to feel as overwhelmed by the reality she is confronting. For the child who's being rejected on the playground, it allows her to see that there may still be a way to get into the good graces of another child. For the child who's scared of anthrax coming into her home, it allows her to see that this is unlikely.

The child who can't do this will struggle when life gets complicated. She's more likely to feel insecure in those situations. This kind of insecurity can even affect a child who seems tough and thick-skinned. A thoughtful, sensitive child may be better at sizing things up and figuring out many ways to solve a problem. The child who jumps in headfirst and is assertive may appear secure, but when life becomes more complicated may feel decidedly insecure.

We see this not only in school-age children, but even more prominently in the adolescent and early adult years. Problem-solvers who can look at multiple causes for things will do better at negotiating the complicated friendships of adolescence. If they are moving into romantic interests, they'll be more skillful because these relationships require a great deal of understanding of other people's multiple motives. Is this particular person not wanting to go out on a date with me because she doesn't like me or because she's playing hard to get? Maybe it's neither and she just doesn't know me well enough yet?" Such thinking is obviously very important in the adolescent years.

Security, therefore, resides in advancing one's ability to resolve difficult situations. To do this requires recognizing the multiple reasons for things as opposed to getting fixated on only one reason, often a highly personalized one. Against the background of a nurturing relationship, parents can help a child wonder out loud whether or not there might be yet another reason for some hurtful experience. When the child can't come up with other reasons, parents can suggest some possibilities and see which one the child favors. When feelings are very stressful and frightening, using this skill requires an even more stable, nurturing context. Deep worries about family members—danger or grief—require trying to see a situation from many perspectives.

Gray-area thinking, like looking for the multiple causes of things, is first learned during the school years between seven and ten. Children are learning to see a range of feelings in their relationships. For example, they can look at another child being angry at them and try to figure out how angry the other child is—very angry or just a little bit. They can size up where they are on someone's friendship list. Not being the first best friend doesn't mean you're not liked at all; it just means you're further down the line. When looking at their own fears and anxieties, not every fear needs to be overwhelming fear; not every fear is catastrophic.

As part of gray-area thinking, and as part of viewing their lives in more relativistic terms, children are also seeing that they are not necessarily at the center of the world, that other people have feelings, too, and that these other people will have relative shades of feeling. If they're a little miffed at someone, maybe the other person will be miffed back at them. Now the child can put herself in someone else's shoes and say, "How would I feel in such a situation?" This skill is not yet fully developed in the elementary-school years and will become more developed as the child enters adolescence. Eventually, when thinking about the dangers of the world, not only can the child think about the multiple reasons why these dangers occur or about how they're different for different groups (the media, the military, or politicians or people in other countries), but she can think about the degree of danger for her family versus others, based on looking at the multiple causes of things.

As with recognizing multiple reasons for events, having the ability for gray-area thinking enables the child to feel secure in a world that's growing more complex. In other words, the world challenges us to understand its complexity and we have to be able to rise to the occasion. There are some things that are beyond children and adolescents, but there's much that isn't. School-age children and adolescents need to be learning these reasoning and thinking skills at earlier and earlier ages in order to understand complex global concerns and not be overwhelmed by them.

### The Ability to Create One's Own Internal Standard and Foster a Sense of Self

As we will see in chapter four, school-age children are learning how to create an internal standard—a sense of themselves and their beliefs. This enables them to compare other views to this standard. So, for example, a twelve-year-old will be able to say and feel that "I'm a pretty nice person. I'm kind to my brother and sister. I know I'm nice even though some of the kids at school treated me like I was awful." A growing sense of self (who we are as people), whether we're nice or mean, bright or less bright, for example, lets the child compare events of the day to that standard.

The younger child (seven to eight years old) is more likely, when she has done poorly on a test, to feel "I'm stupid," or, if someone is rejecting, the child might think, "I'm not very likeable." Once an internal standard is established, however, if it's a positive one, it provides reassurance. If it is negative, however, and, because of life experiences, the child feels "I'm unlovable," "unlikable," or "very, very dumb," then as other things happen in her life to disprove this, she'll be skeptical. She might think, "I lucked out on that test" rather than reconsider her view of herself as not terribly bright. If someone likes her, she'll think, "Well, if they knew how dumb I am, they probably wouldn't like me. Anyway, what if they do. Nobody else likes me anyhow." You can see how the internal standard can be used to shore up a child's security or undermine it.

This internal standard becomes even more important just as adolescence is beginning because the changes of adolescence are enormous. The change in one's body with secondary sex characteristics; the change in internal drives and wishes associated with hormonal changes; the changes in thinking ability; the changes in the scope of one's relationships; the process of feeling more a part of the world and larger community; and the capacity for more intimate friendships, relationships, and sexual interests all make this new ability to shape an internal standard a much-needed attribute. New kinds of risk—illegal drugs, alcohol, unsafe sexual activity—make an internal standard actually of crucial importance.

An internal standard, in many respects, is the essence of what security is all about. Without it, the security one feels is momentary and shifting, depending on what's happening in the changing relationships and events of the moment. If a friend is rejecting, a potential romantic relationship is indifferent, or a job is out of reach, an adolescent can easily feel devastated for a period of time. Such an internal standard can never be absolute, but it must be there to some degree or we tend to see signs of insecurity, such as extreme behavior, doing things just to join the crowd, and many risk-taking patterns. Without an internal standard, there can also be an inability to plan and work toward the future.

Each time interval, from early, mid-, and late adolescence to early adulthood, middle adulthood, and so forth, has new challenges that are well known. The world becomes more complicated. The fifteen- to sixteen-year-old is likely to become interested in dating. The twenty-eight- or thirty-year-old is often interested in having a family with children. These are very different levels of complexity. However, both require this internal standard that can be used to feel secure and deal with the new challenges at hand.

## Security and Empathy

Perhaps one of the most important aspects of having this internal standard and sense of self is that it enables a much higher level of empathy and understanding of others. Now, for the first time, a youngster can truly put herself in someone else's shoes because she has shoes to return to. Children with this ability can think in terms of two realms of experience at the same time. They can think about how they feel. They can think about how the other person feels. They can compare the two and decide how to act.

Consider a concrete example. A group of kids who have been drinking are excitedly talking about the next parties they're going to. Seventeen-year-old Charlie is sitting there feeling the pull to go along with his buddies. He can sense that being as intoxicated as they all are means they don't have good judgment about the road. He empathizes with the sense of power they feel and the sense of excitement they're generating. He also senses how much he wants to go along with them and how lousy he'll feel if he hears that they went to another party, had a great time, and he didn't go. Not having his own car or another ride, he's in a truly difficult position. Here, he must call on another internal standard, one that goes way, way back to his earliest relationships where he established a sense of safety and security for himself. Throughout his growth and development, Charlie was always solving problems and making decisions consistent with safety and security. He didn't walk into traffic. He didn't run in front of the pitcher while he was pitching the baseball. He didn't attack the boy who was twice his size, even though he was angry. This accumulation of experience is now part of his sense of self and he can call on it in a thoughtful way. If he feels strong enough and secure enough, he might even keep his friends from driving to the new party. Even though there would be much protest and little gratitude, at least he could say to himself that everyone was safe, and, as he put it, "They owe me one."

Mature empathy based on an internal standard, that is, stepping into someone else's shoes, seeing how they feel and comparing it to how you feel, and figuring out a workable solution to any conflicts that might be involved, is one of the most important hallmarks of a secure adolescent or adult. An infinite number of social, work, and school situations require this ability. This skill is greatly tested when one has a family of one's own, particularly in relationships with one's spouse and children.

When it comes to dealing with the stresses of the larger world, this internal standard is vital. It enables teenagers and adults not only to assess their own risk more realistically from moment to moment, in terms of relative sense of safety, but also to participate in the discussions, dialogues, and ideas being exchanged to consider how to reduce the causes of conflict and future uncertainty. To do this, one has to be able to look not just at solutions of military and police actions but also at longer-term solutions that require understanding and empathizing with all the groups caught up in any conflict. Planning a safer, sustainable future will involve enormous understanding of the world that goes way beyond what we've asked our youth to do in the past. It will require understanding different cultures, different belief systems, different perceptions of history, and different interpretations of events. Such enormous empathy will be possible only from youth who have a stable sense of self, as well as the ability for gray-area, multiple-cause thinking.

How can we promote this empathy in our children and youth? Particularly, how can we promote it even during times of stress? Here there is no substitute for the basics we've been talking about. Teenagers require relationships with adults just as younger children do, and it is through the discussions in these relationships and the sense of being understood by others that they themselves develop empathetic capacities. In other words, the best way to help a teenager develop a broader range of empathy is to help provide a consistent experience of being understood and empathized with. Parents can spend more time with their teenagers in discussions, in autos driving them places, in family time, or just hanging out and doing some mutually enjoyable things together, whether it's going to a recital or going to an athletic contest or going to a computer show (there are many things kids will take us up on, particularly if we pay). This creates the relationship context for teenagers getting comfortable with us and sharing a little more of themselves with us than otherwise might be the case. When they do share, we have an opportunity to listen and understand rather than close off and give quick, opinionated, controlling orders. ("You shouldn't do that," "You must not do that," "Do this.") If we listen carefully and try to relate what is said to experiences of our own growing up, share those to some degree, and then try to problem solve together, particularly if our teenagers are struggling with a situation in which they're apt to do something that we think is unwise, we're much more likely to get a successful outcome. Empathy for the teenager does not mean going along with what they want or agreeing with their perspective or giving up one's guiding or limit-setting roles. In fact, it enables a parent to carry out these important roles successfully rather than unsuccessfully.

The following chapters will describe ways, beginning in early childhood, that parents can begin to build the basic abilities that lead to a firm inner sense of security and, from that, to a broad, mature empathy. Our children's ability to take over as voting citizens and shape the world in the future will depend on how well we can expand this empathetic range. They will need a secure sense of who they are from which to evaluate other people's experiences and find both common ground and solutions to conflict.

# 3

# Security in Infancy
# and Early Childhood

IN THIS CHAPTER, WE WILL FIRST CONSIDER HOW THE
characteristics of a secure child that we talked about in Chapter
Two are developed in infancy and in the preschool years. Then
we will look at the most common signs of distress and insecurity that can appear during these years and ways to help a child
regain confidence.

## Emotional Foundations of Security

Certain basic emotional foundations for security are laid down
in the early years of life and reworked and solidified during the
grade-school and adolescent years. If these foundations are not
in place, children may run into problems during both early and
later development. When they are firmly established, they con-
stitute a base upon which all future emotional development is
grounded and a sense of inner security can be built.

### Becoming Calm and Attending to the World

One of the first abilities that infants need is to be calm and regulated so as to be able to attend to the people, things, sights,

sounds, smells, and movements around them. By three or four months of age infants should be focusing on what they touch, see, and hear without losing control. Some babies naturally smile and gurgle as they take in the sights and sounds. Other babies—and there are many—have more difficulty. They don't like being touched except in certain ways. Certain sounds bother them. Bright lights make them cry. They are easily distracted, colicky, finicky, irritable. As they get older, they make a fuss if their shoes don't fit quite right or the face you drew for them doesn't have the nose in just the right spot. In school they may not be able to concentrate on what the teacher says because they are so distracted by all the sights and sounds in the classroom.

Once babies are able to focus, attend, and remain calm within their world, they have the first building block of security. Acts as simple as looking and listening and, eventually, figuring out what Mommy or Daddy is saying, or figuring out where a sibling is running to (instead of being overwhelmed), help a baby make sense of the world. A world that makes sense is a world that makes you feel secure.

Alternatively, if this first ability is not well established, the world may appear confusing, unpredictable, chaotic, or simply uninteresting or uncompelling. The baby may either withdraw from it or never get involved in it, instead attending only to his own inner sensations. Or the baby may be exceedingly distractible, overloaded, irritable, and disorganized. It may be hard for him to develop consistent sleep-wake cycles and eating patterns, and eventually to calm himself and learn.

*Feeling Warm and Close to Others*

The calm regulation that makes it possible for a baby to pay attention is needed if he is to become warm, trusting, and intimate with those who care for him. At four and six months, an infant studies his parents' faces, cooing and returning their smiles with a special glow of his own as they woo each other and learn about love together. We see it in a seven-year-old, working independently at his desk, who greets his teacher as she approaches him with a beaming grin and proudly shows her his work. We see it in a twelve-year-old who strolls over to a group of his friends at recess and begins to joke and talk with them, casually draping his arm around one friend's shoulders, playfully punching him in the ribs.

Young children who can't form close one-on-one relationships or group relationships have a fundamental challenge to meet before they can go on to the next developmental level. This is because in the early years of life, most learning comes from what we experience in relationships. Learning to be logical starts with having a smile returned. Also consider how frustration tolerance leads to something as seemingly unemotional as the concept of time. At its foundation, this is an emotional concept because it has to do with the experience of waiting for a need to be met in contrast to getting what you want quickly. This early emotional sense of time is necessary to understand time more abstractly and develop patience later on in life.

When babies feel well nurtured and can rely on the comfort and warmth of their parents or other caregivers, they are taking the first step on this important journey of learning through relationships. This is something that can sustain them in good and bad times. To call on relationships even when you are upset or worried or scared requires a greater degree of trust than does simply calling on them in times of happiness.

With families increasingly stretched for time and both parents working outside the home, the requirements for close relationships—time together, empathy, relaxed intimacy—can easily be lost. Parents need to reassess their commitment to providing the kind of relationships children require.

When a baby forms warm, nurturing relationships, he can use them not only in times of stress, challenge, or conflict, but also to maintain an ongoing sense of security. This is possible because children internalize these relationships. Their sense of being a good person, of feeling important, of being worthwhile and worth being cared for all comes from this experience. Children who don't form relationships and can't trust them generally feel insecure at the deepest level. Relationships are, therefore, one of the cornerstones of enabling a child to feel secure. Alternatively, when relationships are inconsistent or shallow, they contribute to the child's insecurity.

## Communicating without Words

This third foundation for security builds on the first two. (You must be able to focus and relate to people before you can communicate with them.) Between about six months and eighteen months of age children learn to communicate nonverbally with smiles, frowns, pointing fingers, squirming, wiggling, gurgling, and crying. In this way, the infant or toddler is able to assert himself, to take initiative, and to find that his initiative brings a predictable response. The child vocalizes and the parent vocalizes back. The child reaches out for an interesting rattle in the parent's hand and the parent smiles and hands it back. These purposeful two-way communications are the beginnings of the child's sense that he can make things happen. They also establish his sense of reality. When a child can do something to someone else who does something back, he begins sensing where he begins and ends. It's the child who is reaching and it's someone else who hands him the rattle. It's the child who makes a sound and it's someone else who makes a sound back. He gets an appreciation that there is an external reality out there beyond himself. Also during this time the child is learning to initiate and respond to the world of feelings. This will enable him to read the signals of others and express how he is feeling, even without words.

Two-way communication is a building block of many of the characteristics we have described of the secure child. Without this ability, it can be hard for children to form a sense of who they are as people. For example, if they make a sound and no one makes a sound back, or if they reach out with their hand and no one hands them the rattle, they are not getting a response to their messages. This makes them unsure about where they end and the outside world begins. Their sense of self and even their sense of the outside world as a logical place may be compromised. If they keep trying and still get no response back, they may give up and become helpless or passive.

## Acting on the World

A child's sense of being able to act successfully on the people around him is a vital part of inner security. By eighteen months, children become good readers of nonverbal signals and can use these to help them get what they want. For example, when Daddy and Mommy come home from work, an eighteen-month-old will know by their facial expressions or their posture whether they are going to get down on the floor and be playful or whether it is better to wait a bit. He can tell what kind of a mood they are in and gauge his reaction accordingly. At this age children learn to size up a new adult acquaintance as someone with whom they feel safe and who approves of them or as someone who feels dangerous, critical, or rejecting.

Young children who can use and understand nonverbal communication comprehend the fundamentals of human interaction and communication much better than children who can't. They tend to be more cooperative and attentive in school. They are able to pick up on unspoken cues and figure out situations that might baffle other children. Children who have a hard time with nonverbal communication are likely to have a hard time in school and with friends.

A child who can't figure out these cues may distort or misperceive them and is not likely to be able to act appropriately to get what he needs. Being able to negotiate using gestures and eventually words to solve problems has obvious value to the child's feelings of security. When a toddler can find a toy by taking Daddy by the hand, pointing to the shelf it's on, and gesturing for Daddy to pick him up to reach the toy, he is taking charge and solving a problem. He is also understanding how the whole pattern works, how to get from A to D with three or four steps. If Daddy is a willing partner or co-explorer, this problem-solving ability and the initiative it supports takes place naturally. A child who is very good at flirting and getting Mommy to cuddle with him, even when she's busy, is also solving a problem. If he can woo Daddy by bringing him a book and looking up at him with wide eyes, he is likely to win Daddy's heart and, even if Daddy is busy, convey to him what's most important. On the other hand, a demanding crying child pulling Daddy when Daddy isn't sure what the child wants is likely to result in a tense Daddy. This may result in a child that gets angry or annoyed, or passively goes along without much enthusiasm.

Obviously, this ability does a great deal to help a child feel secure. He doesn't have to wait and hope; he can create his own security blanket, so to speak, by problem-solving with his caregivers to get what he wants. If this is to happen, they have to be responsive, particularly in the early years. As a child gets more verbal, he can try out different adults if one adult doesn't respond. A toddler, however, is dependent on a parent or other caregiver to be the collaborative partner, thereby strengthening this skill.

When a child is not mastering these capacities, we see the seeding of insecurities. The child who doesn't, for example, see the steps it takes to get from A to D, who can't figure out how to get his toy that's on the shelf or can't figure out how to express his anger short of biting or throwing a full-blown tantrum, is at a decided disadvantage.

The ability to work with others to get what he wants gives a child the confidence to operate in a complicated world. The inability to do so can arouse tremendous feelings of insecurity. Unless the demands of his world are very simple, the child who doesn't have these skills won't be able to meet them. At a minimum, children must be able to communicate through facial expressions and, later, words that they are worried; and they must be able to find ways to draw their parents into offering comfort and security. This might be as simple as a child figuring out a way to get his father to spend more time holding him, even while he watches the news.

*Putting Emotions into Words; Using Ideas*

A child who says, "I want that bear," instead of just grabbing it, is using symbols. When children say, "Give me that," or "I am happy," or "I am sad," they are substituting a thought or an idea for an action (kicking or hitting). They not only experience the emotion, but they are also able to experience the idea of the emotion, which they can then put into words or into make-believe play. Children who can do this begin to exercise their minds, bodies, and emotions as one. We can see children using emotional ideas in make-believe play—for instance, if the dolls are hugging or hitting or explorers are racing excitedly to the moon. The ability to use fantasy underlies much of creative thought. When children are asked to make up a story or to figure out how another child might feel or to understand the meaning of a story that the teacher is reading, they are being asked to make certain creative leaps based on this ability.

Many children (and adults) continue to have difficulties with this ability. They equate feelings or thoughts with action: "If I think it, I will do it." They may avoid pretend play or verbalizing feelings, fearing that by acknowledging feelings, they'll act on them. In general, I've found, children who have difficulty controlling their aggression often have difficulty acknowledging feelings to themselves and then expressing the idea of those emotions through words. Instead, they get right into action, discharging their feelings through their motor system—hitting, biting, pushing. Sometimes a child's anxieties and conflicts cause this difficulty. Other children never acquire the ability to express their emotions in the first place. They haven't learned to formulate the thought or feeling as a way of delaying or pondering their course of action. They can't identify and label their intentions and feelings and, thus, are unable to hang on to them long enough to think of a different way to express them. Children who can't identify their intentions and feelings and who have an action-only oriented approach to life are more apt to use aggression as a way to cope with challenging situations.

To see if your child is capable of expressing his emotions, look for a situation in which something of his has just been taken away by another child and ask, "How do you feel when that happens?" If the child just swings at the other child or says, "I'm going to kick him!" he's not giving you evidence of using an emotional idea. If the child, however, says something like "I feel mad!" and when you say, "Well, what do you feel like doing when you get that mad?" he says, "When I get that mad, I feel like hitting and kicking," then he has reached the stage where he can form an emotional idea around a feeling.

Children learn to use emotional ideas through day-to-day experience. Spontaneous communication gives children practice in using and listening to words that are tied to their motivations and feelings ("I want that toy now!"). When children hear others use words to express their emotions in certain contexts and then experience the same emotion, they try the words out. If their efforts are greeted with empathy and are amplified upon, it strengthens the connection of that word or concept to the feeling.

Many of the characteristics of the secure child rest on having this type of ability. To be able to discuss all of these feelings is of enormous help, especially during times of stress. The child who can use ideas is able to play out these feelings in pretend dramas as well. The child who is scared can pretend to be strong. He's going to be a policeman and put the bad guys in jail. Or he finds three big bears who are going to protect him. Either way, the child is working something out mentally to help overcome feeling helpless and scared.

## Connecting Ideas and Thinking Logically

Between the ages of two-and-a-half and three-and-a-half, children make connections between different categories of ideas and feelings. "I'm mad because you didn't come and play with me," or "I'm happy because George was nice." This means connecting two feelings across time and recognizing that one is causing the other. Again, we see this in make-believe play: Children start to develop plots—one set of ideas and another set of ideas connected up. For example, a child's dolls will fight—not just randomly, but for a cause, because a car was stolen by bad people and now the good police are getting it back. Such an ability to connect ideas on an emotional level underlies all future logical thought. As their ability to build bridges between ideas grows, children become able to reflect on and categorize their personal emotional experiences. Human thinking reflects a person's emotional experiences; as mentioned earlier, our concepts of time, space, and quantity, as well as our likes, dislikes, and opinions, always begin with subjective experience.

At this stage, children begin to make the distinction between fantasy—things that are "inside me"—and reality—things that are "outside me." This ability enables them to control their impulses and plan for the future. "If I do something bad to someone else, I may hurt him, and I may get punished." They begin to understand that the world works in this logical way; actions have consequences.

Contributing to the child's ability to develop these thinking skills are his unique physical characteristics (for example, the way he reacts to and processes sensations and organizes responses), his environment, including family, community, and culture, and his interactions with his caregivers and peers at each stage of development. These skills can be mastered in many different ways, and different cultures often have their own unique approaches. One should not mistake these developmental processes for specific beliefs or ideas. We are talking about helping children learn to relate, communicate, and think, rather than about specific beliefs. It is important to emphasize that through respecting each child's physical and cultural uniqueness, we help him understand and think logically about the world.

This ability to connect ideas in a logical way is another cornerstone of feeling secure and making oneself secure. The child who can do this can figure out how the world works and what he needs to do to change the situation that is making him scared. He can figure out that if someone he encounters looks dangerous it's best to find an adult he can trust. Most children intuitively know this, but in a time of extra stress the child who can figure this out for himself is more likely to find a game plan or solution.

This ability for logical thinking helps with a sense of security in many other ways as well. It's the building block of judgment, of planning, and of most academic skills. As we will see in the next chapter, it helps children negotiate with peers.

In other words, for a late preschooler (a three- to five-year-old) to be able to participate fully in his life activities of preschool, peer friendships, and family life, and to learn about numbers and letters, he needs the ability to think. When he has this ability and it is developed very strongly, he can apply it to new situations that are scary and stressful.

To help a child who is not developing logical thinking, engage him in long, opinionated conversations where you help give his opinions. We will have many examples of this at the end of this chapter when we talk in more detail about how to promote these core capacities in infancy and early childhood.

These are the six building blocks of security for infants and preschoolers. We will now look at what can happen when these building blocks are not solidly established or when the stresses are so large that children develop anxiety, distress, or symptoms that they cannot fully manage. We will identify the most common and important ones to look for and then discuss how to alleviate them.

## Common Signs of Distress and Insecurity in Infants and Preschool Children

Infants and preschoolers will generally reveal a sense of uncertainty through varying types of feeding, eating, and behavior problems. They will sense anxiety through their parents' reactions, rather than through an understanding of the events. Preschoolers will, however, be taking in images and playing them back in their pretend play and verbal expression. In this section, we will look at the types of behavior that indicate a child is feeling stressed or insecure.

### Excessive Sadness

Some children, particularly older preschoolers, may look excessively sad when they are worried. A child may assume the worst and prepare for it by being sad ahead of time. He may be worried about his mother or father not coming home or something happening to himself at school. Instead of showing worry, he's showing sadness.

This is a child who often requires extra nurturing care and lots of support. He needs a great deal of involvement along with a great deal of practice in being assertive and in problem-solving. This child also often may have lots of anger that he is not expressing, and therefore in pretend play one should offer opportunities to express such feelings, particularly when bad things are being done in the play. Over time, with extra nurturing from parents, opportunities to take charge, and help with expressing anger, often the sadness slowly retreats. We begin to see a spark emerging in the child's eyes. Of course, if family patterns are contributing to the worry and sadness, these need to be understood and worked on.

## Aggression and Excessive Risk-Taking

Some children become impulsive and aggressive in a destructive way. Others become more active and risk taking, jumping off of high places without knowing where they are going to land and running out into the street. Still others may become insensitive to the needs of other children, taking their toys, for example.

When this pattern becomes worse due to stress or has become an established pattern, the key is firm, gentle limits, and emphasis on more interaction. This child needs lots of warm communication so that he begins responding more to other people's cues and the cues of the environment. This will help him to make better judgments. Games called "regulation games," in which the child runs fast, then slow, then superslow, or plays the drums loud, soft, and then supersoft, can help. By modulating and changing behavior in this way, the child learns to regulate himself more and more.

## Excessive Fears and Anxieties

A child who is generally very sensitive will become especially so with new stresses. The child may want constant reassurance and be very clingy and needy. He may be coming into the parents' bed at night and may be verbalizing dangers that seem out of proportion to the stresses around him.

To help this child parents can work on two fronts at once: provide extra nurturance, security, warmth, and opportunities for expressing feelings; and work with the child to gradually become more assertive.

## Avoiding Certain Feelings

Some children respond to stress by narrowing down the feelings that they are willing to express with gestures or words or play. They may, for example, be very comfortable talking about how much they love their daddy or how much they like another child but avoid sharing feelings of anger or annoyance. Some kids can express feelings of fear but can't express sadness or disappointment or rejection. They may verbalize a fear of being hurt by someone or of someone taking them away but not express fear of their mommy being taken away. Children will differ as to where their vulnerabilities lie and which feelings they avoid. New stress tends to reduce the range of feelings a child can put into words. Sometimes the feelings that are avoided may be directly related to the stress. For example, in a time of stress children might talk about scared feelings but be afraid to mention angry feelings because they are afraid that their anger might mean that their parents won't protect them. Parents can consider whether or not a child is able to express the full range of human feelings—closeness, anger, fear, anxiety, worry, joy, curiosity, and so on.

Parents or caregivers can use pretend play to broaden the range of feelings. After establishing a rhythm for a number of weeks with pretend play, the adult may respond to something the child does with a behavior that would evoke the avoided feeling. For example, let's say the child is scared to talk about anger. When the bad guy takes the doggie from the good guy, the adult might inquire, "How do you feel that I took your doggie and what do you plan on doing about it?" In other words, you don't press the issue but you provide opportunities for the child to practice verbalizing some of the feelings he is scared of.

## Fear of Putting Feelings into Words

Some children, particularly when scared or anxious, find that putting a feeling into words makes it more scary. It's as if the words make it more real, in comparison to just showing it with a facial expression or a gesture. When some children are very scared, they may approach you, look scared, and indicate they want to get a hug, cuddle, or protective embrace. But even if they are otherwise verbal they have a hard time saying, "I'm scared." They are frightened that the words will make the feeling worse, so they shut down any verbal expression that relates to certain feelings.

For this child it's important to try to reduce any source of stress. It's important to provide a safe setting to help this child gradually take the chance of verbalizing his feeling and see that it's not so scary after all—that it actually helps him feel a little better. The best way to do this is again through pretend play. Dolls can use the scary words. After three or four weeks of pretend play you might try asking if he feels just a teeny little bit scared or a little bit worried, and he may just nod his head, "Yes," which is a beginning. Eventually he will be able to say the words, too, and develop a whole new skill.

## Physical Complaints

When under lots of stress, some children develop headaches, tummy aches, or other physical symptoms. These are often experienced by the child as real discomfort. Part of the reason that this occurs is that the child doesn't to have the ability to use emotional gestures to show you how he feels or can't attach words to his feelings. The child then expresses the feeling physically. Some children are more likely to do this because they tend to have more sensitive stomachs or get headaches easily. Many of the techniques we've already discussed are also useful here.

## Fragmented Behavior

When under stress, many children behave in a fragmented way, jumping from one toy or activity to another. They don't seem to have an organized pattern of behavior that allows them to look to the caregiver for permission and organize their behavior in a way that furthers their goals. Stress and fear can certainly make this pattern worse.

Here, the key is to set firm, but very gentle, limits on the impulsive behavior and to start getting the child to be more purposeful and more organized. This child often requires lots of interaction or encouragement to focus on an action or follow through with a thought. We will be describing how to do this in the next section.

## Passive, Helpless Behavior

Some children, when they are anxious or fearful, retreat into helpless passivity. This is most clear with a toddler or preschooler who cries whenever he wants something and is easily overwhelmed by any frustration. He seems to want everything done for him. The helplessness sometimes is expressed as excessive demands. The child threatens a tantrum whenever you don't do what he wants. This is a pattern that most parents are familiar with, but what may not be so obvious is the fact that stress or anxiety can make this pattern much worse.

The key here is to help the child become more assertive. This can be as simple as letting him hand you a toy rather than your going and getting the toy or letting him reach up on the shelf for the book he wants rather than your taking it down for him. You can act dumb and get the child to gesture for you to pick him up and then encourage him to reach it for himself. Challenging the child to take initiative takes a lot of support, help, and warmth. Of course, if there are overwhelming fears and anxieties, reducing those and providing more basic nurturing time together are also obviously very important steps.

### Freezing Emotions

When a child freezes his emotions it is not as obvious as when he withdraws from people. Such a child becomes scared of expressing feelings with facial expressions and gestures. His expression does not change. He does not reflect happiness or sadness, glee, sorrow, excitement, or curiosity. By the time children are eight to ten months old they show all these different emotional expressions. These gradually develop from about three or four months on. A child who has just one expression is freezing his emotions. If he can't express his feelings with facial expressions or other gestures, this may limit the degree to which he can actually feel them inside. Sometimes overwhelming fear, as you might see in abuse or neglect, or lack of opportunities for expressing and exchanging feelings can lead to this worrisome pattern.

To help this child, a parent must go back to the basic building blocks of security that we discussed earlier. It is important not only to woo the child into relating but also to engage the child in exchanges of emotions, beginning even with basic smiles and then moving on to other emotional expressions. Any type of interactive game (rolling balls to each other or making funny faces at each other, for example) is great to improve communication. If a child has been abused or neglected, a comprehensive program for him and his family, planned by professionals, is needed.

### Withdrawing

A child may withdraw from other human beings if he experiences them as relatively unavailable or not consistently available. If there is abuse or neglect, he might experience care-givers as frightening. When feelings are especially overwhelming for infants and toddlers, they can in extreme cases withdraw from the world and relate only to their own body. Such children try to stimulate themselves with little regard for what's around them. We see this in institutions where children are neglected or ignored, but it can also happen from overwhelming stress.

In such circumstances a comprehensive program is needed. As part of this program it's important to woo the child into relationships and if the child does have some special problems, such as being overly sensitive to things like touch or sound, to approach him in a way that's comforting and regulating and enhances his sense of security. (See *The Child with Special Needs* and *Infancy and Early Childhood* for more information on this challenge.)

## Helping Infants and Preschool Children Strengthen Their Sense of Security

In this section we will discuss in more detail ways in which to help our infants, toddlers, and preschoolers feel more secure, even in difficult situations. These strategies are also useful even when there are no problems, just to strengthen the core abilities that maintain security described in Chapter Two. There are three basic kinds of help: the unstructured time together that I call "floor time," problem-solving, and gentle, firm limits. Each of these kinds of support must be tailored to the child's physical makeup.

### *"Floor Time"*

"Floor time" is when you interact with your child on his terms, following his lead and helping him learn to engage with others, communicate, and begin to think logically. Each of these abilities, as we have seen, contributes to a child's sense of security. Many parents do all of this intuitively. Others will find it useful to follow the steps described here.

*Following a Child's Lead, at His Level.*   The main principle of floor time is a simple one: A parent gets down on a child's level, and the child is encouraged to be the boss of all the drama that unfolds. The parent follows.

A small child's world is largely on the floor, where he feels most comfortable and where his toys and playthings are located. When you get down there with your child, you generate a sense of equality that encourages him to engage with you, take initiative, and act more assertively. However, "floor time" can also mean operating in the child's realm by making funny faces at him as you change his diaper, chatting at meals or while doing errands, splashing in the tub, or walking outside. Thus, "floor time" can occur anywhere and anytime you and your child are interacting in a way that lets him know that you are joining him at his own level. This home ground consists of his interests, initiatives, and ideas.

*Let the Child Choose the Activities.*   Any kind of playful sharing is valuable as long as both of you find it enjoyable. If you wind up occasionally choosing the game, try to encourage your child to take the lead and play at his own pace.

Each parent may prefer a different type of play. One of you may enjoy fantasy play, while the other may enjoy art projects or physical activities. It's fine to have different roles, as long as each of you is an enthusiastic participant. Your child will sense what you enjoy, and expect different types of play with each of you.

Floor time is neither a time for teaching nor an occasion to get controlling and bossy. Floor time is the one arena in which it's safe to let your child be the boss. Even eight-month-olds want to be in charge of their own play. Only two limits are necessary: no hurting people and no breaking toys. These can be implemented gently but firmly.

With a baby, feel free to join in on whatever he is doing at that moment: clapping, making noises, or playing with a rattle. As you follow his lead, imitate his gestures and emotional tone with your own expressions. Share his smiles and pouts. Most importantly, entice him into a little dialogue of gestures with you.

If a preschool child is painting or building with blocks, gently try to join in. If he insists that you watch him paint a picture, follow his suggestion but try wondering aloud if you could paint a little, too. If he winds up telling you five reasons why he is a better artist than you, and that you should just watch him at work, this is still floor time and the theme is "I'm better than you."

The closeness that is established by regularly joining the child in his own interests and at his level will become an essential part of a child's inner security.

*Shared Communication.* When you make it a point to follow your child's lead and build on his interests and overtures, he will usually be inspired to respond to what you do or say. I call this process "opening and closing circles of communication." If your child moves his truck and then you move your car next to it and say "Where are we going?" you're opening a circle of communication. If he then builds on your lead by saying, "We go to house!" or simply bangs his car into yours while giving you a knowing look, he is closing that circle of communication. Your play partnership encourages him not only to take the initiative but also to respond to whatever you add to the game. Even when a child says only "No" or "Shh!" he is closing the circle of communication. This ability to tune in to another person in a continuing dialogue is one of the core abilities that leads to a sense of security.

*Creating an Appropriate Play Environment.* One way to facilitate a child's ability to open a dialogue with you is to provide a

sampling of simple, age-appropriate toys, such as dolls, action
figures, cars, or blocks. You and your child can use these together to pursue his natural interests. You can help bring such
props alive. When you pick up a stuffed frog, speak in a croak;
as you push a toy car, make "vrooming" sounds. In this way you
will be using them to promote creative interactions between
the two of you.

Some children do better with a few select toys, while others
enjoy using lots of toys. Dolls and action figures make it easier
for many children to explore in fantasy some of the real situations and real feelings, some of which may be frightening, that
they experience in everyday life. Floor time gives them a safe
place to experiment with scary feelings. Board games and puz-
zles tend to create more structured rather than spontaneous interactions.

*Extending the Dialogue.*   The best way to extending your
child's communication with you is to interact constructively
with him by helping him toward his goal. For example, you
might notice that your eighteen-month-old is pointing at a toy
elephant on a shelf that he can't reach. When you reach the toy
and ask, "Want it?" and he reaches for it with a big smile, you
are helping him reach his goal and at the same time extending
his interaction with you.

If your two-year-old is bashing dolls together, you could first
acknowledge his activity with a comment like "What a huge
fight!" Then you could put a puppet on your hand and say (in
the puppet's voice), "I'm watching the fight!" If your child
shows an interest in your action or, better yet, tries to take the
puppet to break up the fight, you can expand the activity still
further by asking whether he needs another puppet to help.

Playful obstruction can also get some joint action going. For
example, if he's avoiding you, you might try positioning yourself
between your child and the toy that is absorbing all of his attention. You can be the fence or mountain that he needs to

climb over or under to reach his favorite truck. If your child seems determined to move his toy cars on his own, you can try covering one with your hand to create a "tunnel." He may be motivated to search for it by picking up your hand. All this can keep the play from falling into rote or solitary activity.

*Allowing Aggressive or Angry Feelings into the Play.*     Floor time allows a child to explore all the marvelously varied themes of life: closeness and dependency; initiative and curiosity; affection and aggression; and pleasure and fear. There will be times, however, when you'll notice that your child will neglect certain types of themes, despite your best efforts to create a supportive floor-time environment. At those times, it's appropriate to introduce gently those emotional areas that he seems to bypass. For instance, if your three-year-old tends to be a little passive or timid when it comes to asserting himself by claiming his own toys, you could move his favorite truck away from his group of vehicles. Make sure you've got a big grin on your face as you move the car away slowly and deliberately in a non-threatening manner. Your three-year-old may very well assert himself and come after his prized truck!

If your child's floor time seems preoccupied with themes of anger or aggression, try not to interfere by asking questions like "Why is [the character] so mad?" or "Why can't [the character] stop fighting?" Instead, you might say, "Gee, he really wants to smash those bad guys and finish them off. He must be really angry about something!" By acknowledging both the anger and the fact that he must have a good reason for it, you are showing him that you are on his side rather than being critical.

The imaginative and verbal expression of feelings usually helps a child learn to understand and regulate them. Strong feelings such as anger that aren't acknowledged tend to get acted out either directly, with the child becoming aggressive, or indirectly, as he reacts in an opposite manner and becomes overly inhibited or fearful. Your acknowledgment of your child's feelings does not imply approval for acting them out in reality. Instead, your words will help him use ideas rather than actions, and strengthen your ability to discuss and set relevant limits on aggressive behavior.

A child who can express and regulate his angry feelings will be a more secure child. If you convey an empathetic message that it's okay to explore aggressive themes during play, dependency, love, and concern will usually emerge, too. Otherwise, his frustration at being misunderstood may cause him to polarize his feelings. His anger and fears may feel overwhelming to him.

*Strengthening a Child's Confidence in His Muscles and Senses.* Floor-time play can appeal to many of a child's senses and involve the muscles of his body at the same time. These can work together as he interacts with you in an emotionally meaningful and fulfilling manner. Try to introduce visual and spatial elements into the play. See if he can see under a door or spot you hiding behind a nearby chair. In a similar manner, spatial play such as building forts and towers with blocks can also broaden your child's range of processing and motor skills. Perhaps he'll want to build a city. You could become his assistant architect or construction worker. Cities need someone to deliver food, to provide security, and to make sure that the monsters don't get inside. Extending your child's abilities as he plans the games and follows his dreams will help give a child a sense of competence, a sense of himself as a person who can accomplish things. We'll see more of that in the discussion of problem-solving below.

*Group Floor Time with Siblings or Friends.*   Sometimes, it's difficult to engage in one-on-one floor time, and parents or other caregivers will be working with a few children, siblings, or playmates. There are two ways to get group floor time going. One is simply to let each child be the leader for around twenty minutes with the other children being actors or props in the leader's drama. Everyone follows the leader, whether it's playing school or good guys versus bad guys. The adult's job is to help the nonleaders follow along with the drama as it develops. Even toddlers can be included as fellow actors. They may run with you to hide in a closet or sit in your lap while you're being served tea. A nine-month-old can be assigned a role as a friendly alien by an imaginative four-year-old astronaut. When it's the nine-month-old's turn to lead, you and the other children can simply try to open and close circles of communication with him. A four-year-old pretending to be "Mommy" might hand a nine-month-old sibling a rattle and see whether he will reach for it.

A second way to get group floor time going is to let the group find a common theme to engage in. This approach can work for three- to five-year-olds or older children who play cooperatively. In this sort of group floor time, the adult subtly helps the children discover shared interests and initiate their dramas and expand them. Themes ranging from playing house or school to exploring space to reenacting cartoons may get the drama going, and the children will use their creativity to move it down interesting paths. The adult then has the pleasure of watching true improvisational themes unfold.

Both group floor-time approaches have the same goal: to help everyone get involved and to interact. In this way, all participants are attending, engaging, being purposeful, using lots of gestures, and, when it is age appropriate, creating ideas and logically connecting them. Most important, adult and child get to have fun with each other.

### Adapting Floor Time to Each Child's Individual Profile

Successfully interacting with your child during floor time means adapting the play to his individual developmental profile. The following are five different profiles that may describe (alone or in combination) your child.

- *The Easily Overwhelmed, Sensitive Child.* Some children are sensitive even to light touch, certain sounds, bright lights, or abrupt movements. As you play with a sensitive child, he may be very cautious and may need lots of time to adjust to something new. He may also have a special need to be the boss of all the action and to control others. Children with sensitivities naturally want to test the waters of life only one toe at a time, and need to be wooed into pretend play gradually. It's vitally important to respect his need to be in charge, and to let him use your playtimes together as a way to experiment gradually with assertiveness and become more confident
- *The Underreactive Child.* A child who is slow to react may be reluctant to assert his will by gesturing, using words, or playing "let's pretend." Such a child needs to be wooed into activity. Over time, little spurts of curiosity or interest will lead him to step into make-believe roles. Eventually, he may relish ordering his parents around the room in an active rather than passive manner. Often such a child may need to manifest assertiveness or aggression through gestures and pretend play before being able to express it with words.
- *The Child Who Craves Sensation.* With very active children a parent's task is twofold. First, "go with the flow" and build on his natural interests, but then also hold his attention and help him to elaborate on his interests rather than jump from one topic to another. Otherwise, his craving for new sights, sounds, and touches may lead to frenzied, aimless behavior, rather than to active and organized play. Once such a child is focused on a theme he has chosen himself, he may be able to sit down and concentrate for fifteen minutes or more. Try to mix in "modulation" games, going from fast to slow, noisy to quiet, to help him learn to regulate his behavior. A very active child may need extra soothing, and affectionate handling, as well as encouragement in the use

of ideas as well as actions. A child who feels himself losing control is not a secure child.

- *The Child Who Takes In Sights but Tunes Out Sounds.* Some children have a harder time than others figuring out what certain sounds are and often find it difficult to pay attention to their parents' words. Rather than simply naming objects or pointing to pictures in a book, parents can use floor time to give lots of extra opportunities to practice understanding words. Pretend games in which a child is naturally motivated to do the "talking" for dolls or action figures are natural ways to support verbalization. Chatting with your child when you know he really wants something helps him pay attention to sounds, too.
- *The Child Who Takes In Sounds, but Has a Hard Time Figuring Out Sights.* Some children have the opposite difficulties. Treasure hunts, building things, and the use of visually exciting props during pretend play are all useful with such children. In play, they may be motivated to pay more attention to visual detail.

## Problem-Solving

In addition to the freewheeling fun of floor-time play, special one-on-one time for problem-solving is an important way to build feelings of security. In addition to the routine daily challenges at home or preschool, these sessions can focus on the "big" issues that your child may face: waking up at night, toilet training, hitting other children, throwing food on the floor, temper tantrums, or being mean to a sibling. Fifteen- to thirty-minute chats—ideally not in the midst of a crisis—that take place over a period of days rather than a big one-shot discussion are most helpful.

If a preschooler is strong-willed, he may well spend the first ten minutes ignoring you, changing the subject, or flatly announcing, "I don't want to talk about it." It's important to realize, however, that it may take fifteen minutes of discussion for the child to recognize your genuine interest. Of course, not every child is this reluctant. Some will debate an issue for hours.

Once you introduce a subject, try to listen to your child and empathize with his perspective: "I bet you could tell me lots of reasons why you think it's okay to pinch." Eventually he may give you his list of complaints: "He grabs my toys" and "You always take her side." The more clearly you understand where your child is coming from, and the more you give him a chance to verbalize his complaints, fears, and wishes, the better chance you'll have of not only resolving the problem but helping him grow emotionally. Don't assume you know what your child thinks and feels. And even if you do know, he needs to say it. Let him do the talking. Nodding or mumbling yes or no answers to your questions doesn't help him with better problem-solving skills. The child who likes to talk the least needs to practice this skill the most.

Some children have difficulty seeing the "big picture." Even highly verbal and logical children may often become overwhelmed with their feelings of the moment. If your child has this problem, you can draw his attention to the larger patterns that he's overlooking. Other children have a hard time describing details or recognizing shades of feelings. Encourage him to reflect on his experience: "Tell me what happened this morning; I have lots of time." Your interest in the particular aspects of his feelings will help your child avoid overgeneralization. If your child is unable to picture a situation that will happen tomorrow, help him picture it and discuss how he will feel. As he becomes older, this skill will help him face situations that appear forbidding or scary.

### Limit-Setting

The third important step in building a child's sense of security is to establish firm limits. The special times we have described for building relationships have to be coupled with clear, consistent limits. These steps must go together. When you eliminate one avenue of expression—your child's impulsive or disobedient behavior—always give him another way to express his concerns. Successful limit-setting melds warmth and empathy with a rock-solid resolve. A child who grows up with such limits will feel safer, reassured by a world that is predictable and makes sense.

*Mobilizing Your Resolve.* Frequently, parents lament that their child "just won't listen." He won't get dressed, pick up his toys, etc. And yet most children don't scribble on the living room wall more than once, because their parents have a firmer sense of resolve when it comes to having to repaint their walls than when they must pick up toys. Most children recognize the areas where their parents' resolve is clear, and generally only misbehave when they think they can get away with it. So the first step in limit-setting is deciding which limits are really important to you and sticking to them. Resolve is communicated not only through words but also through gestures.

*Teaching Limits.* Limits are taught, not dictated. Your child's transgressions will provide you with plenty of teaching opportunities. Once a child is able to understand gestures, as well as a few words, you can get right in front of him and firmly shake your head from side to side as you say "No, no!" You can then aim his torso away from the temptation and reiterate "No TV!" or "No lamp!" while he toddles away. He may cry in frustration, but your persistent use of head shaking and resolute-sounding "No!"'s will show him that you're not going to give in.

Toddlers gradually come to learn what your words and gestures mean, as they associate words, actions, and affects (feelings) with each other. On the other hand, if you simply pluck your child out of harm's way because it is easier (although in obvious danger you will of course do whatever is expedient), he will learn only that being picked up means "I can't do something," but will not learn respect for your words and guidance. Actively look for opportunities to teach when you and your child are on familiar turf and not in a public place, like a store, where you will be afraid of causing a scene. When you ask your child to pick up his toys, eat with a spoon and not his hands, get ready for bed, share toys with a friend, or put on his shoes, you'll have a chance to do some constructive teaching. Ask yourself the following questions:

- Have I my child's attention?
- Does he understand what I want? Are my words or gestures clear enough?
- Is he is paying attention and does he understand me but is choosing not to obey? Am I motivating him enough with positive regard, including respect? Am I prepared to motivate him with a reasonable sanction if needed?
- Should I be more persistent and firm, and can I be gentle but firm if physical restraint is needed to protect my child from danger or from hurting someone else?
- Have I been making regular opportunities for empathy and dialogue through daily floor time and problem-solving?

If the answers to these questions are all "yes," the limits you impose should be readily learned by your toddler.

*Maintaining Empathy, Involvement, and Dialogue during Limit-Setting.* The natural human tendency is to pull away from empathy and closeness when you're involved in angry exchanges, power struggles, or limit-setting. How can you empathize with misbehavior? You can empathize with how hard it is to learn new lessons, for instance, to see a nice toy and not grab it. It is only when limit-setting is coupled with empathy that your child will eventually wish to please you. After all, your goal in setting limits is to teach greater empathy and respect for others, and your child will learn from what you do more than what you say. Nevertheless, many parents naturally find that they long to escape from their draining, angry children. If you give in to this feeling, however, the escape pattern you set up will succeed only in making your child feel even more rejected, vulnerable, angry, or frightened. Your best approach is to take charge and reestablish a sense of security and control. Extra floor time and a focus on problem-solving will also help. After a few weeks of reaffirming these special moments, setting firm limits on your child's angry whining is both appropriate and helpful. Empathy, rather than escape, will help to reverse the cause of your distress.

*Choosing Your Battles.* Part of setting limits is deciding what to limit. This isn't easy. Your own values and family situation will lead you to choose, but then you must be willing to set the boundaries clearly and enforce them. Focus on just a few key issues at a time. It's better to win a few important battles with sound teaching than to lose lots of little ones out of exhaustion. For instance, work on "no hitting" and leave cleanliness for later. Don't make the tactical mistake of waging a war on three fronts at once or establishing very narrow categories for permissible behavior.

For example, don't punish your child for specific, narrowly defined kinds of transgressions, such as hitting, biting, or pinching. Instead, focus your discussions on the larger category of "respecting other people's bodies and not hurting people." The issue of "respect" and "not hurting" will cover any clever or lawyerly twists your child can come up with to defy you, such as "But I did too obey you! I didn't hit, pinch or bite. I just shoved him really hard." Your goal is to help your child deal with general principles of behavior and see the whole forest rather than specific, niggling details.

*Reasonable Sanctions.* Try to look for punishments that aren't developmentally detrimental. For instance, try to avoid restricting playing with friends, because that activity is too valuable. Consider alternate sanctions like no television, no computer games, an earlier bedtime, or KP duty. Children need punishments that challenge them. After a parent I knew imposed a fifteen-minute time-out, his four-year-old said frankly: "That won't work. It's too easy!"

Time-outs are not necessarily effective. They can suggest to your child that you are not able to withstand his anger. Going eyeball to eyeball with him or even asking him to think quietly in your presence about what he did may communicate greater resolve on your part. More important, some disobedient children have maturational lags, which limits their ability to comprehend what you say to them. They "tune out" and can get lost in their own fantasy world. The last thing such a child needs is social isolation, which would permit him to daydream even more, and would further undermine his ability to test what is real and what is not. The child may experience time-outs as only mildly annoying or even pleasurable, making them an ineffective way to set limits. It is the child's ability to balance intimacy, trust, and respect with anger that will lead to self limit-setting. Methods of punishment should never be cold or mechanical or lack the very empathic values you are trying to teach. Constructive limit-setting takes place in the context of a warm, respectful relationship.

*Avoiding Overprotection.*    Some parents are too fearful of or pained by their child's discomfort to set meaningful limits. If you find yourself backing away from effective limits, try to discuss these feelings with your spouse and explore the roots of such feelings in your own past. Instead of watering down your discipline, try to do something much harder: Deal with your own inner pain and guilt over the situation by offering time together to your child. After all, you can't give your child too much of this! Then, make sure to choose a limit that is genuinely meaningful to your child. Because every child is different, you'll have to experiment and see whether a disappointed, stern look from you, days without television or a favorite toy, or an earlier bedtime will prove to be more convincing.

*Tantrums.* Tantrums create a whole range of feelings in parents: mortification at public embarrassment, hurt feelings, frayed nerves, or panic.

Tantrums serve different purposes. There is a big difference between the child who cries at every little thing because he is overtired or getting sick; the child who wails in frustration because he can't tie his shoe; or the child who is uncontrollably angry because you won't let him eat a chocolate bar right before dinner. Knowing which kind of tantrum you are dealing with will help you handle it.

The overtired child needs you to help him calm down by holding or rocking him, or reading or talking to him, or by drawing his attention to the colorful flowers outside the window. The goal is to teach him that even when he is really upset, he can settle down. Try not to feel that "I'm being manipulated" when your child is overtired and fussy. He simply needs your assistance in helping him feel calm and regulated once again.

When your child becomes frustrated because he can't do something he is trying hard to do, realize that his tantrum is similar to the anger you yourself may experience when you hit your thumb with a hammer as you try to hang a picture hook. There are occasions in life when a person is entitled to ventilate! Firm limits are necessary, however, if your child becomes destructive and tries to hurt someone or break something. For instance, if your child flings his shoe directly in your face out of frustration, it's certainly time to set a limit.

Because most of us have sympathy for our fellow adults' moans and groans when they can't do something like figure out their new computer software, why not extend the same leeway to our own toddlers or preschoolers? Try to empathize with your child's frustration and outrage over ornery shoelaces or complicated toys. Then, after he calms down, see if he wants your assistance. If not, cheer him on from the sidelines as he tries again.

When your child throws a fit because you won't give him what he wants or let him do what he wants, this is time for strict limit-setting. Most parents find these sorts of displays of anger the hardest of all, especially if their child is strong-willed and they themselves are sensitive to loud noise or angry feelings. The most effective way to avoid these tense times is to first make sure that there is ample warmth, closeness, nurturance, and respect in your relationship with the child and then to supply him with many opportunities to communicate his angry or frustrated feelings. It is important to establish a track record of limit-setting for earlier, serious infractions, such as hurting a sibling or violently throwing toys.

As far as the tantrum itself is concerned, first acknowledge the situation. "I understand you're mad because you didn't get what you wanted." Then, steel yourself to wait out the tantrum until the child is able to communicate—in words or gestures and not just by crying—why he feels that you have been unfair. The tantrum will only escalate if you yell back, try to defend your position after you have made it clear, try to bribe him with compromises, "jolly" him out of his angry facial expression, or banish him to his room because you can't stand to listen to the racket he's creating. Let him understand that if he chooses to let you know how mad he is by using words (or gestures, for a little child) you are ready to listen. If the tantrum brings out a tendency for self-injury (biting or banging), for breaking things, or for hurting you, you'll have to institute some immediate and firm limits. Containing him firmly in your arms will often do the trick. In such instances be prepared for a real workout!

Once you combine limit-setting with extra floor time, your preschooler may generally become warmer and more cooperative, but his tantrums may get more intense for a while. Any child will resist giving up his means of protest! But in time the tantrums will subside.

*Teaching New Coping Strategies during Limit-Setting.* Besides limits, your child needs to find new ways to get his needs met and to feel a sense of self-respect rather than humiliation. By the time he is two, you and he will exchange words as you teach him how to use ideas in the heat of battle. Emotional ideas are a big advance over simply yelling, crying, or pouting— all of which are characteristic of earlier stages. Similarly, when you and your three-and-a-half-year-old have a twenty-minute discussion in which he contends that watching extra TV is a better idea than going to bed on time, your limit-setting negotiations are teaching him complex emotional reasoning. By entertaining his arguments you are not being a pushover; if he doesn't succeed in persuading you, you can still insist that he go to bed.

It is relatively easy to discipline your preschooler when he covets and then swipes another child's toy. But it is harder to figure out what needs your child may be trying to meet by taking something that belongs to someone else. Perhaps his greediness stems in part from a hectic home life in which he feels insecure. His greed in this case may arise out of an attempt to feel important and respected. The question then becomes: "How can I help him feel proud and secure in other ways? How can I help him realize that his interests, skills, silly jokes, and feelings of frustration and loss are important?" Whenever there are serious challenges to limits, you can bet that your child has unmet basic needs concerning such things as the parental relationship, sibling relationships, or problems caused by his own physical development.

If there is a single golden rule for limit-setting, it can be summed up in a few words: Give more and expect more. The amount of affection and empathetic interaction we offer our children has a clear connection with their ability to rise to challenges or meet the demands we make of them.

Although it may sound simple, this advice is not easy for many of us to follow. As I mentioned earlier, there is a natural tendency to pull away when children disappoint or frustrate us. In the face of defiant disobedience, perhaps to stifle an intemperate response, we may pull back, walk away, and occupy ourselves with chores. We may even mumble to ourselves, "After all I've done for him, he won't even . . ."

In such a situation, a child not only feels the pressure of your expectations but at the same time also feels less nurtured. This double whammy will probably make him feel angry and frustrated. If he could clearly articulate his dilemma, he'd utter something to the effect of "What? Pick up my toys? When you won't even pick me up and cuddle me?" In general, a child will respond more enthusiastically to your heightened expectations—whether it's picking up toys, curbing aggressive tendencies with peers at school, or learning to share—if he feels he is receiving ample amounts of soothing "emotional chicken soup," coupled with firm but gentle limits and guidance.

The key to a feeling of security in infants and preschoolers is to build up the child's basic abilities to relate, express, and read emotional signals, and to use his gestures and ideas to solve problems and think logically. Rather than leaving the child to fall back on aggression, withdrawal, or tantrums when he feels stressed or insecure, we try to help him advance to better ways of coping with fear and anxiety.

# 4

# Security in the
# Grade-School Years

THE GRADE-SCHOOL YEARS PROVIDE OPPORTUNITIES
for children to develop additional kinds of competence that enable them to feel secure. If they haven't yet mastered all the
basic skills discussed above, they will need to continue to work
on these while they confront the challenges of grade school.
During these years, children achieve three basic new abilities.
We will first explain how these contribute to a sense of security.
Then we will outline the most common signs of insecurity and
distress in grade-school children and ways of helping children
overcome them. Next, we will also discuss some ways of adapting our "floor-time" principles to the grade-school years.

## New Abilities That Help Build
## Security and Confidence

### Triangular Thinking

From about four-and-a-half to about seven years of age, all
things seem possible. Kids at this age have a curiosity about life,

are bold and expressive, and show a deep sense of wonder about the world. Most place themselves squarely at center stage. They want everything to be enjoyable. They're willing to work, as long as it is fun and exciting. Some find letters and numbers pretty boring, while others readily love the challenge of learning. Motor coordination improves at this age—throwing, kicking, skipping, jumping. Improving fine-motor coordination means children can do such things as tie their shoes, learn to write the letters of the alphabet, and draw shapes such as squares, triangles, and diamonds.

As you probably already know, this stage is commonly called the Oedipal stage: Boys, it is suggested, have sexual fantasies about their mothers and girls about their fathers, and children develop strong rivalries that coexist with loving feelings toward the parent of the opposite sex. Less well known is that this phase ushers in a new type of relationship: a triangular one. Mother and father are no longer interchangeable, as they were when the child was younger. The child now plays out all sorts of rivalries and intrigues. A boy may strive to impress his mother at his father's expense by saying, "Daddy, get out of here!" Soon after, the roles may shift. Such behavior can be very upsetting to parents. It helps to recognize that this is one of the ways a child figures out more complicated types of relationships. Having three people in a system gives a child greater emotional flexibility. Now the child's relationship with her parents is triangular instead of one-on-one. She doesn't have to look at the relationship with each parent as an all-or-nothing situation. If her mother is a little aloof at times, a child can woo Daddy, hoping Mommy will get jealous, instead of despairing and crying as she might have done earlier. Or if her father is just now uppermost in her affections, she can pretend to ignore him and act coy, sitting next to her mother while waiting for him to win her over. This may be a time for parents to readjust the balance in relationships. A busy father, for example, can make himself more available in order to give the child two people to depend upon.

The ability of children to see the world in triangular terms buffers the intensity of their feelings and provides the security that comes with choices. If a boy is angry at his mother, for example, he can express his anger without fearing (as he would have earlier) that he might be abandoned. Now he can imagine that he and his father are comrades-in-arms, going on an all-male adventure together. In reality, obviously, the boy isn't ready to let go of his mother, but at least he now has the flexibility in fantasy to play out different dramas based on his triangular system. In a typical family, children already have a primary dependence on their mother and need to become more independent of her. By relying more on father, they feel freer to explore and try themselves out, while still feeling secure. An alliance with father also helps buffer the strong feelings children may have toward their mothers. Fostering triangular relationships is, of course, easier in a two-person family. But children in a single-parent family will also learn to seek out and experiment with triangular relationships. For example, they will use siblings, friends, teachers, or their parent's love interest— whoever is available to create triangles.

During this time, the most important task for two parents is to solidify their fundamental alliance. The child needs to realize that no matter how hard she may try to get one or another parent to be her primary ally, the parents are firmly allied with each other. Parents who drag their child into marital difficulties by pulling her over to one side or the other create unnecessary insecurities for that child.

These same patterns repeat themselves with your child's friends, real or imagined. A five-year-old, for example, might have two imaginary friends to boss around—she referees their fights, corrects their table manners, and decides who gets to go on car trips with Mommy or Daddy. Imaginary friends can satisfy some of the wishes of children, standing in for the loyal follower, or the needy, vulnerable person whom the child can protect. Real friends can also absorb some of the feelings of dependence a child has toward her parents. She may want to see a certain friend all the time and may talk about him or her constantly, as if holding on to the relationship for dear life.

During these early grade-school years, children can still get lost in fantasy and thoroughly enjoy it, but can usually differentiate between fact and fantasy. While riveted to cartoon programs, they probably realize that these are not an accurate portrayal of the world.

At the same time, these years can be a time of great fearfulness. Their new sense of power and rich fantasy life can easily frighten children. They may fear ghosts and witches under the bed or robbers coming to kidnap them. While their sense of reality may be strengthening, they may have little islands of belief in magic, as in "Witches could be real. I don't think they're real, but they could be real."

In contrast to the grandeur they display at home, children at this age can revert to being coy or shy in new surroundings. Parents may be surprised when their intrepid five-year-old clings tightly or will not sleep in a strange room.

If all has gone well, children emerge from this stage with certain abilities that will help them remain confident in the face of new challenges. They are able to grasp more complicated relationships and, in this way, become more emotionally stable. They have begun to develop a capacity for more "adult" emotions, such as guilt or empathy (although empathy is easily lost when they are feeling jealous or competitive). And they can experience and express a wider range of emotions and emotional dramas—revolving around dependency, rivalry, anger, or love, for example. All of these abilities equip children to move securely out from their families and into the wider world.

In summary, this stage of more complex and triangular thinking helps a child feel secure in several important ways. First, it leads to a sense of grandeur and power, which supports earlier experiences a child has had of having an effect on the world. This gives her a positive, optimistic outlook and motivation to figure out how to solve problems. This more sophisticated thinking offers solutions other than yelling to get your way or hitting to get even. An ability to see the world in terms of greater complexity is essential for a child trying to figure out her place in an uncertain and stressful world.

The key way to help a child achieve more complex thinking is through discussions that seek alternative explanations. Have a flexible family structure so that you don't get upset when a child seems to manipulate others to get her way. Appreciate that it's a far better way of coping than just throwing a tantrum. You may not give in when she manipulates, but you can still appreciate the fact that she's being cunning and clever in her attempts to get an extra Christmas present by, let's say, talking about all the great presents her friends have gotten. That's far better than whining, and even if it makes Mommy or Daddy feel guilty, they should respond with appreciation of the cleverness that went into it. This encourages an attitude that encompasses the world's complexity.

### Thinking in the Emotional "Gray Area"

In the seventh and eighth years, children begin to move from the family-oriented stage of development out into the rough-and-tumble world of peer relationships. They move away from triangular relationships at home and enter the multifaceted world of their peers, immersing themselves in the politics of the playground.

Many new skills develop at this age. Motor coordination improves even further—children can jump rope, for example, and throw a ball, catch it, and throw it back fairly accurately. They write more fluently and can now draw figures of people that are more realistically proportioned. They understand many interrelated ideas and concepts, and can communicate more clearly their wishes, needs, and fantasies. They can now categorize numbers, shapes, friendships, etc.

At this stage, some of their rich fantasy world fades and they are more likely to pretend to be a police officer controlling the bad guys, for example, than a Ninja warrior saving the world. No longer so expansive and grandiose, their focus now is on mastering the skills they have learned.

Children's self-image now begins to be defined by the group—by the pecking order that prevails on the playground—instead of being determined solely by their parents. In everything from athletic ability to popularity to looks, brains, and clothes, children rank themselves against others. At this age, children can tell you with amazing accuracy who is the best reader, who tells the biggest lies, who runs the fastest, and who is the most popular.

Initially, all this doesn't mean they don't feel loved or valued by Mommy and Daddy. They are beginning to see a new reality. They can be unpopular even if they are loved and valued by their parents. They rate themselves within the group based on what their friends think, and their self-esteem soars or plunges accordingly. As much as parents want to reassure a child that she is a sweet, adorable person whom they love, life can still be painful if, for example, she is not invited to a certain birthday party.

To negotiate successfully the intricacies of multiple relationships within a group, children now have to learn to reason on a very sophisticated level. This ability helps children to develop cognitive and social skills that will be very valuable in school and beyond, because much of the world they will eventually operate in will involve shifting social relationships. Most of life operates in shades of gray, not in all-or-nothing extremes. A child begins to see that feelings and relationships can exist in relative terms. She can be angry at a friend but still want to be invited over to her home. This ability to see the world in relative and more complex terms translates into advances in schoolwork as well, helping children to grasp math concepts and themes in literature. They are now able to fit into orderly pat-

terns of relating to others; for example, they learn to follow the
rules of Little League baseball or soccer.

Despite this new maturity, many children don't accept disappointments or loss gracefully. They can't accept that a friend
doesn't like them, learn to live with that fact, and move on to
other friends. They hold on, taking the loss as a personal defeat.

As part of their desire to make sense of their world so as to
feel secure in it, older children can go through times of being
overly rigid and orderly in some areas (for example, perpetually
arranging shoes or books) while being quite sloppy in other
areas (handwriting or eating habits). New worries arise, such as
unrealistic appraisals of their physical appearance, so that they
feel ugly or unattractive ("My nose is too big" or "My hair is too
curly").

Competition can be very intense. Games are taken very seriously ("You cheated, I know it!"). Children may be intolerant of
anyone other than themselves changing the rules, and may take
a loss personally. At this stage, humiliation, loss of respect, and
disapproval may be a child's worst fears.

School-age children gradually learn about their position in
the group and, to some extent, in the larger culture. The new
experience with gray-area thinking and playground politics fosters the children's appreciation of complexity and multiple
causes. This enables them to face more complex problems, thus
shoring up their confidence in making their way in the world.

Also, the ability to understand gradations and shadings of
feelings allows the child to have much more stable relationships
and to use those relationships constructively. A child can see
that some people meet *some* of her needs some of the time and
others meet them *more* of the time. She can understand how
relationships work and whom to seek out for what kind of help.
A secure person is one who can figure out the world and understand how emotions and relationships work. When a child
can't do this, she will feel insecure for a variety of reasons. She
may have trouble with friendships because she can't appreciate

the complexity of school relationships and what to expect from which friend. She will be upset when someone seems to ignore her and overly expectant when someone is nice to her, not understanding that the seeming meanness was only inadvertent and the seeming niceness was only manipulation. The child in this situation will be insecure because she will constantly feel disappointed by misguided expectations.

Children who can't appreciate shades of gray tend to lapse into polarized thinking. If this becomes extreme, it can interfere with their understanding of reality. They may become convinced that everyone hates them or that all schools are dangerous places.

Parents who use shades and gradations in their own thinking and ask children to express their feelings in shades and gradations are preparing children for this stage of development. "How much do you want that particular birthday present?" There are many opportunities in the family for these kinds of discussions. Mostly, however, gray-area thinking is reflected in the way a whole family approaches feelings. Is the child all good or all bad, or has the child just been a little bit rambunctious? Children in families that tend toward all-or-nothing thinking will have a hard time with this stage.

*Internal Standards and a Growing Sense of Self*

From about the ages of ten to twelve, children begin to develop a more consistent sense of who they are. Gradually they are better able to develop an inner picture of themselves, based on who they feel they are rather than on how other people treat them. They begin to shape their own goals and values and become a little less influenced by the issues of the moment. When this is achieved it is, as we have seen, one of the characteristics of a secure child.

Children derive this internal picture of themselves from interactions with family, friends, teachers, and others in their lives. Their growing ability to see the world in more relative terms allows them to hold in mind an emerging sense of their inner selves even while being buffeted by relationships within their peer groups. They can now hold on to two realities at once: their peer group reality and their emerging inner reality of values and attitudes. Both internal values ("I shouldn't be mean") and future goals ("I want to be a teacher someday") now take shape.

These inner standards help strengthen and stabilize children's self-esteem at this stage. They are more able to see life in perspective. ("Maybe I'm not the best player, but still I made the team.")

In the physical realm, kids can now engage in sports that require strength as well as muscle coordination and skillful hand-eye coordination (including perceptual motor skills), such as basketball, football, and tennis. Their writing is more fluid, and they're able to handle intricate manual tasks, such as taking things apart or using a screwdriver.

The rapid physical changes children undergo as they approach puberty may affect their schoolwork. Formerly gifted students may suddenly appear forgetful. On the other hand, some children who have been diagnosed as slow learners may suddenly start getting As and Bs as parts of their nervous system mature. Lipstick, dirty jokes, sneaking into R-rated movies, and increased shyness around the opposite sex are all part of the eagerness for, and fear of, the physical and sexual changes about to occur during puberty. As children begin to mature sexually, they may develop an increased interest in role models and (for a while, at least) a closer relationship with the same-sex parent. This is a time when a father can really develop a special relationship with his son, and a mother can nurture her relationship with her daughter. At the same time, ten- to twelve-year-olds are not reluctant to criticize their role models.

These years on the cusp of puberty are a scary time for children, as they begin to contemplate greater independence from their families. Rocked by strong feelings, they may feel caught between their childhood longings for closeness and dependency and their desire to grow up and be teenagers and young adults. Sometimes they seem bold and defiant—"Who needs you?"—yet at other times they're clingy and insecure. Only their solidifying sense of themselves will gradually make life more stable. Without it, they may slip back to depending even more on parents or try to deny their dependency by taking more risks or becoming more rebellious.

Rather than facing the challenges of independence or dealing with the opposite sex, children this age may focus instead on their bodies: Girls may complain of stomachaches or headaches; boys may focus on the size of their penises or their muscles. Negative feelings about their bodies are not at all unusual.

Just before puberty, the capacity to empathize—the ability to put oneself in someone else's shoes—really takes off. Kids are more capable of empathizing with a friend who has been rejected or who has hurt feelings. They feel loss and disappointment more keenly. They now experience an adult-like sense of sadness that shouldn't be trivialized. While, earlier, when a friend moved away or a grandparent died children were able to talk about feeling sad only occasionally, now they mourn such losses deeply.

New cognitive abilities allow children to derive their motivation internally rather than from friends or family ("I want good grades so I can go to college," rather than "Mom says do math homework tonight or I'll get into trouble"). Their consciences, rather than the ever-present parental eye, begin to provide them with more moral guidance. "I didn't study and was mean to my best friend." They have a greater concern with right and wrong, perhaps developing an interest in societal issues that involve people being treated unfairly. They are also more capable of understanding and following rules without outside guidance.

At the same time, it is easier for a child at this stage of development to rationalize breaking the rules. That's because along with this greater concern with right and wrong come more sophisticated reasoning powers. For example, when scolded for not taking a rule seriously, a child can rationalize that "grown-ups get too serious and need to mellow out sometimes!"

The internal standards developing at this age are essential to feeling secure. The child can now operate in two worlds—the changing outside world and the world inside her, which takes on a more stable quality. The child's internal sense of security is associated with a picture of herself. This image is no longer just little pieces, but is now more integrated. "I'm good at some things and no good at others, but I'm someone who likes to learn new things, which is good." A child can see that some schoolmates like her and some don't, and in spite of this feel generally likable inside. This inner sense of self provides reassurance in different areas of life, whether it's schoolwork or peers or family life. It's an essential ingredient for approaching the more complex problems life will bring in adolescence and adulthood. It builds on any security that has been achieved at earlier ages.

When this inner standard isn't there, a child is vulnerable to feelings that switch with every momentary shift in relationships. Children are much more vulnerable to going along with the crowd, doing things that they know their parents disapprove of—even things they disapprove of themselves—when they don't have this inner standard by which to evaluate temptations. When security comes from acceptance by others, a standard that will change from moment to moment, a child will feel buffeted and vulnerable. We all need some of our security from outside affirmations, and so do children during this stage. But children who have an inner standard are able to supply a healthier percentage of this sense of security themselves, which gives them a degree of stability that the children without it don't enjoy.

## Signs of Insecurity in Grade-School Children and Ways Parents Can Help

There are many common signs of distress in grade-school children. As we examine them, we will also offer ways to turn each of these varied signs of distress into new strengths and coping skills.

### Excessive Fears and Worries

School-age children will often have more intense fears and worries than their preschool counterparts do. This is because they can now more fully appreciate a danger seen on TV or covered in the newspaper or overheard from parents. The danger isn't just a fleeting image, as with a preschooler; it's one that they can hold onto and examine. However, children at this age don't yet have the tools to assess this danger in terms of the likelihood of it happening to them. This ability won't come until adolescence. They know too much but do not yet have the coping capacities to deal with what they know. For children who tend to be sensitive and anxious to begin with, this can sometimes lead to worries serious enough that help from parents and others is called for. Perhaps the child is talking all the time, for example, about whether her parents will be safe if they are away on a trip. Sometimes the excessive fears and anxieties come out in nightmares or in fears of going to sleep, or fears of sleeping alone, or of kidnappers coming in, or of bad people doing something harmful to them. The fears will seemingly be unrelated to the stress that produced them. After the terrorist attacks in New York City and Washington, D.C., many children were having fears of being kidnapped as well as nightmares about all kinds of calamities. They didn't necessarily relate these to the disaster they had seen on TV. In other words, the mind continues the theme but changes the characters.

To help a child whose fears are excessive, it's important to work on a number of fronts at once. Parents can provide extra security and protection, extra warmth and nurturing, extra time and opportunities to express feelings, and, most important, they can provide factual reassurance and opportunities to help others. An overly fearful child may have long-term problems with assertiveness. Often she may be very frightened of aggression. Extra practice can foster an assertive attitude, whether it's calling friends for play dates or arguing with a sibling. The chance to help other people—reassuring small children, or writing letters to a friend who has lost a family member or companion animal, or perhaps doing errands for a frail, older person—can be especially helpful to a child.

### Excessive Sadness or Depression

Acute or chronic stress can lead certain children to become sad, and this state of mind can shift into depression. Children may feel that they can't do anything right or that they are bad. Sometimes the depression takes the mild form of the child's simply not wanting to do anything. In rare cases, it can also take a more extreme form in which children declare that they wish they'd never been born or may even attempt to hurt themselves.

When a child shows signs of depression, a parent can handle the situation in much the same way we described for the child who is fearful and worries a great deal: nurturing, factual reassurance, and opportunities to express feelings and to be assertive. When a child talks about a particular situation, it's not useful to argue about the illogic of her sad feelings. It's best to listen carefully, empathize, and when possible raise alternative ideas for her to consider. Remember that you cannot control the thoughts in a child's head. Therefore, reason and understanding, not arguing, are best. If the sadness or depression becomes extreme or doesn't respond to a parent's efforts to help, then professional consultation should be sought.

*Problems with Learning and/or School Discipline*

Many children respond to stress by finding it hard to cope with some of the more challenging settings in which they find themselves. For many children, school is more challenging than home. School requires a child to sit still for many hours a day, concentrate, learn new and sometimes difficult lessons, and be disciplined. There are often far more rules in school than there are at home. In such a setting, it's easy for a child to demonstrate her distress by having problems with learning or conforming to the rules. If the child's behavior changes abruptly—one who was a learner has all of a sudden stopped learning, or one who had been reasonably disciplined in school begins acting up a little more—be aware that a recent stress may be a factor. It is important to distinguish a long-term pattern of difficulties with school from one of a temporary change in behavior.

Aside from the basic steps in creating a feeling of security that we outlined in Chapter One, it's helpful for the child to feel that her parents and teachers are working together to help her. This may mean giving her more time for homework because she is preoccupied and doesn't work efficiently. It may mean reducing homework assignments or some of the academic demands temporarily so she can get back into a situation of mastery. It may mean gentle support to help the child attend or control her behavior. The idea is to keep the child from feeling overwhelmed. School challenges can gradually be restored once the child has calmed down and is able to work at her earlier pace. This approach is more likely to be helpful than trying to be overly firm and discipline the child or insist that she carry the same load as before.

For the child with long-term learning and/or behavior problems that get worse due to recent stress, the same principles apply. This assumes that the child has had a full evaluation and that a comprehensive program is in place. (See my earlier books

*The Challenging Child* and *The Child with Special Needs.*) Children feel more secure if they see that they are making progress.

## Overdependence on the Crowd

While we more typically see the pattern of overdependence on the crowd in teenagers, it actually begins during the elementary-school years. Some children have a hard time focusing on what they feel is right and wrong and want to do everything that everyone else does. They want to dress like the other children and have the same book bags. During the nine- to twelve-year age range, this pattern can get very intense. In extreme cases, children may not fully develop a sense of who they are and, instead, follow the crowd in every way. Sometimes this syndrome results in the child being rude because the other kids are rude; at other times it plays out in a child throwing tantrums if she can't have exactly the hairdo or exactly the clothes other children have. The child, in essence, is trying to use belonging to the crowd as a way of enhancing her security. Just as some children become dependent on their parents during these times and become clinging, other children become more dependent on their peers. They seek to do this by using peers as their "security blanket."

When this pattern is excessive, it usually suggests that parents may need to reinvolve themselves in the child's life, with floor time and problem-solving discussions as well as gentle but firm limits. In this way such children can find more security with their parents and have more balance in their lives. Renewed closeness will also enable them to talk about some of the frightening or anxious feelings that may be making them too dependent on the crowd.

## Extreme Self-Centeredness and Bossiness

All children are more or less self-centered, at least some of the time. But some children insist that everything be done their way. This can involve controlling how their friends play with their toys, who gets more time with parents (themselves versus siblings), how much dessert they get, and so forth. This can become a chronic attitude of the child who doesn't appreciate the feelings of others.

Children often become self-centered as a way of reassuring themselves that they are O.K. In other words, the focus on "me, me, me" is a denial of feeling vulnerable. It's as though they were saying, "If I get all the attention, and everything I want to eat and to play with, maybe I won't have to feel like I could lose it all and have to feel so vulnerable."

For the child who is responding to stress this way, it's important to help her become aware that by trying to get everything on her terms, she is running away from a feeling of vulnerability. This can be done only gradually. It often involves a combination of lots of warm time together, lots of gentle limit-setting, and helping the child see the relationship between vulnerable or scared feelings and being self-centered. For example, "You know every time we talk about the plane crash, you ask me for extra candy. I feel better when I have candy, too. But it doesn't take away the feelings. I understand, but sometimes we need to talk about scary feelings, too!" Such a dialogue can occur against a background of a warm relationship with consistent nurturance and limits.

*Taking Everything Personally*

There are children who tend to respond to the normal shoving in the lunch line by declaring that some child next to them deliberately hit them. These children may personalize any uncomfortable experience and feel that it was somehow purposefully done to them. Such children are more likely to worry that something they read in the newspaper or saw on TV will bring harm to them or their mothers or fathers.

In helping children who personalize a great deal, it is important to determine whether this reaction is predominately in response to stress or an intensification of a pattern that has been there all along. In either case, it's important to help such children see that while scary things that are out there in the world could happen to any of us and that we all worry about them, there are many, many people in the world, and bad things usually don't happen to everyone. Such children often need help in understanding the needs of others and, more generally, the perspectives of others. They need assistance in reaching out beyond themselves and seeing that they are not the only ones in the world—that not only does the candy and cake need to be shared by everyone, but everyone is worried about bad and scary things, and we can all help each other. This realization is a gradual process.

## *Polarized and Rigid Thinking*

As we saw earlier, during school-age years children are generally moving from seeing the world in all-good or all-bad terms toward the acquisition of gray-area thinking. Children with rigid, polarized thinking feel that everyone either loves them or hates them. They may think they are brilliant or completely stupid. In other words, their emotions tend to go from one pole to the other. Some children, when facing acute stress or ongoing anxiety, regress to polarized thinking or use it more than they do when they are feeling calm and relaxed. When a child who has begun to master some gray-area thinking slips back into rigid extremes, she may be feeling a high level of stress and anxiety. Seeing the world in simpler terms is a way to cope with this.

In such a circumstance, it is important first to listen empathically and help the child express a little bit at a time what she is scared about, then to work on more subtlety in her thinking. Be patient and help the child articulate how the kind of feeling she is having compares, for example, to one she had yesterday or the day before. This will encourage comparisons and facilitate gray-area thinking: "Well, I was not quite as angry today as yesterday," or "Today I'm even more angry than yesterday." Also, talking about feelings in subtle ways in the family and making feelings a topic of conversation help the child learn that feelings occur in gradations and shades, as do the thoughts that accompany them.

### Fragmented Thinking

When a child is unable to organize her thoughts into a coherent, logical conversation, she is probably also fragmented in her thinking. She will jump around from one topic to another without ever quite finishing her thoughts. There are no transitions from one subject to another. Rather than saying, "This cartoon character is really funny. Oh, that reminds me of Uncle Tommy, who had a red hat, too," the child might mention a cartoon character and then a character from another TV show and then talk about what she wants for dinner, and so on. This type of fragmented thinking is sometimes characteristic of children whose thinking skills have not progressed. They still think like children who are first learning to use words, when it is natural to jump around quite a bit. When fragmented thinking happens to a child who has a well-established capacity for being logical and coherent, it suggests a fairly high level of stress or anxiety.

Here, again, it's very important not to criticize the child or insist the child make sense, but rather to listen warmly and empathically and to try to help the child find how she got from A to B. For example, you can wonder out loud, "Gee, I was trying to listen but I got kind of lost. You were talking about frogs and now you're talking about popcorn. How do they go together?" That simple question provides a little structure for the child to try to find some bridges between her ideas that will make her communication more logical and coherent. For the child who is responding to stress, it is also obviously important to provide opportunities to express feelings about what might worry her and to provide the kind of nurturing security we've talked about before.

If a pattern of fragmented thinking continues over a long period of time, a professional consultation to figure out if there are additional causes is appropriate. Sometimes children will be more vulnerable to this pattern when they have some processing problems, like a weakness in the way they take in sounds and words or a weakness in the way that they comprehend what they see. This could then be exaggerated under acute stress or high levels of anxiety.

### Escape into Fantasy

Like preschoolers, school-age children can enjoy escaping into fantasy. Consider a nine-year-old, for example, who, when a difficult subject comes up about school or about scary feelings or about a family conflict, begins getting silly. If there are pretend play materials available, she starts to play with the materials on her own, talking to different dolls or characters or action figures. She may release her feelings by banging the toys, or become involved in a self-absorbed elaboration of a fantasy. While it's important for children to have time to express their fantasies and they should be supported in this, we should also help them return to reality. In doing so, if children are using fantasy play as an escape from dealing with a difficult important element of reality, it is important to approach that subject gradually and slowly.

Here, the best strategy is to be very supportive and warm. Draw the child's attention to the challenging issue and then give her room to practice her escape-into-fantasy act (she won't give it up very easily). Join her in her fantasy play so that she feels your support for that side of her life. Sometimes gently draw her attention to what she seems to be running from. She will begin to see the pattern and it will gradually be easier for her to stay with a reality-based conversation. Some children will escape into fantasy even when there is no immediate stress. Other children will do this only in response to something that's difficult. The child who does it all the time, without any immediate stress or difficulty, requires a longer effort to bring her back into the everyday world.

## Denying Feelings

Feelings are an important part of the way we communicate and think about ourselves and others. Therefore, when a child shuts down this part of life because the feelings have become scary, she is giving up more than she realizes at the moment. School-age children typically will deny feelings or rationalize feelings that they are uncomfortable with. They may just simply say that they feel fine and that they don't think about the scary events that everyone else is thinking about. ("Please leave me alone so I can play my computer games.")

The key here is not to pressure the child or keep insisting that she is having feelings just because everyone else is. Rather, look for a back door into the child's world of feelings by hanging out with her. As you talk with the child about what she is interested in, gradually the world of feelings will become more accessible. Over time, there will be opportunities for the child to begin sharing a little bit. A child may initially come up with the idea that you are a terrible computer game player, and she's going to give you instruction. If you allow her to flex her muscles and be the boss and enjoy your company on her terms, she will begin feeling more secure. Later on, if the family is talking about a recent frightening event, she's more likely to join in and perhaps take a chance in sharing her feelings, at least a tiny bit. This is a gradual process for the child who tends to deny feelings, requiring support and nurturance and a chance to enjoy relationships with her parents, particularly during playtimes, on her terms.

## Narrowing the Range of Feelings

Many children don't deny or shut down feelings, but they do narrow the range—for example, showing affection, but not real warmth, or expressing anger, but not compassion. They may empathize with a friend who is hurt, but not one who is competitive. Here, the same types of interaction we discussed above for denying feelings are often helpful. As you build comfort and security, you can gradually stretch the conversation and interactions.

## Physical Symptoms

Like preschool children, school-age children can also channel their fears and anxieties into physical symptoms, such as stomachaches or headaches. The key here is not to get into an argument or accuse the child of making up physical symptoms, because for her they feel very real. In fact, they *are* real in that the child usually feels a great deal of actual discomfort, even though the initial stress may be psychological.

The key is to provide lots of outlets other than physical symptoms for expressing feelings. The child needs help in being able to label, express, and demonstrate feelings of all types. That will lead to putting the current stress into words. You can support the child's description of her physical symptoms and listen carefully for clues such as, "It feels like somebody has hit me in the stomach." Perhaps someone has been mean or aggressive. "It feels like six people are sitting on my head." Perhaps the child feels lots of pressure from parents or teachers.

*Impulsive and/or Disorganized Behavior*

This is a very common reaction for some children when they are anxious or overwhelmed, particularly for those who tend to be active and assertive to begin with. When they get scared, instead of growing more cautious they tend to become impulsive and chaotic in their behavior. For some children, this can take the form of being aggressive with siblings by pushing, biting, hitting, and hurting; for others, it can take the form of being a bully on the playground; and for still others, it can take the form of misbehavior in class, getting up when they shouldn't, speaking out when it's not their turn, refusing to stay in line, and so forth. While it can take many different forms, the common denominator is impulsive and disorderly behavior.

If this behavior was a problem before any new stress, the child requires a full evaluation to look at the underlying causes, such as whether there is a problem with planning and sequencing behavior, or with attention or language or visual-spatial thinking. It can also be related, sometimes, to a very low threshold for pain and other sensations. The child is constantly seeking out more sensation. An evaluation can provide a more complete picture. During the time that parents are learning more about her behavior, they can begin by gently helping the child put her feelings into words, and recognizing and working on her behavior. It is also useful to set up firm and gentle limits and to play modulation games, like those described for preschoolers (any activity where the child has to modulate behavior).

For the child who is responding to a particular stress with impulsive behavior, the same program may be appropriate, but may not need to be carried out as long or intensively. One can observe how various parts of the program are working for the child. Problem-solving conversations and discussions of how to anticipate future challenges tomorrow are also helpful strategies.

*Passivity and Helplessness*

Rather than clinging to parents, school-age children often express their helplessness by giving up easily and finding every new task and challenge beyond their capacities. This could apply to chores around the house or even activities that one would think they would enjoy, such as peer play dates or pursuing hobbies.

If the quick retreat is not an ongoing characteristic of the child, it can be a sign of stress or anxiety. Passivity and helplessness are ways of coping with frightening demands. Often there is an underlying wish for someone else to make everything O.K.

Whether this is a chronic pattern or a response to stress, the child needs gradually to learn to become more assertive. This can begin with seemingly small interactions at home in which the child is helped to take charge of things that are manageable. It may be doing one homework problem on her own and then getting help from Mom or Dad. It may be putting a few socks in a drawer as a prelude to cleaning up the mess in the room. Start small and focus on encouraging the child's initiative. For this type of problem, it's very important to create a context of extra security and warmth.

*Freezing Emotions*

When under stress, school-age children, like younger ones, can become very inhibited about expressing their emotions, not just with words but even with gestures. They become hard to read. They look stone-faced. The emotions seem frozen. This, too, can be a sign of either long-term stress or reaction to some recent trauma. The child feels that she has to put a strong control on all her emotions, including the expression of them.

This is a worrisome sign. To remedy the situation, it is important to provide extra support and to nurture and then build up to interactions that are animated and involve lots of dialogue and feelings. Unless the child feels secure in her relationships, it's unlikely that she'll feel safe enough to begin showing her emotions. It should be pointed out that some children have difficulty showing their emotions with facial expressions for physical reasons. For example, there is a rare malady called Mobius Syndrome in which children have difficulty moving their facial muscles. Some children with severe developmental problems and low muscle tone also may have more difficulty with facial expressiveness. It is important, therefore, to look at other ways in which such children can express emotions, such as their body posture, movement patterns, and tone of voice. Children with physical limitations who are comfortable with a range of feelings often find ways to convey them. It's especially important to notice a lack of expression in children who were previously emotionally expressive and then have shut down, as well as to recognize when children never developed their emotional expressiveness because of chronic stress.

Besides the warm, nurturing, and animated interchanges that should be instituted, the parents of children who freeze feelings should look at the stress level within the family, and their own availability for relaxed time together.

*Withdrawal*

As we have seen, grade-school children are usually preoccupied with the politics of the playground and their peers. Withdrawing from relationships often means withdrawing from the challenge of the peer group. Instead of trying to play with friends or being in activities where kids their own age can be found, they may engage in more solitary activities; in the extreme, they ignore parents as well as peers. When withdrawal is more limited, it may involve only the avoidance of new challenges in peer relationships. Children may elect to use computer games, TV, or hobbies as an excuse to withdraw from the essential challenges of the grade-school years.

To help kids get reinvolved with peers, it's important, first, to draw them back into a relationship with parents and through that into a range of age-appropriate activities. Keep an eye out for activities that are so consuming that they undermine the child's ability to have a balanced interest in the challenges of the world around them. This might be any number of hobbies, for instance, collecting baseball cards to the exclusion of all else. Parents can initially show interest in baseball cards or computers or TV or whatever else is preoccupying the child, and then broaden that interest into things that will actually be more fun when done with friends.

Parents can then gradually begin arranging (or helping the child arrange) play dates with other children. Initially, it could be together with Dad on a weekend when the child and her friend go to some activity that she loves to do, whether it's a computer fair or a zoo or the playground. Once the child sees that having another kid around might not be too bad, then parents can begin working to identify children at school or from other activities who might be called for play dates. Sometimes parents will have to be there orchestrating the play date and creating activities until the child gets the hang of it. Be patient and look for gradual progress. If a child doesn't begin making progress, a professional consultation may be needed.

## Increasing Security in the Grade-School Years: The Five Principles

We've made some brief comments about ways in which parents can help children with specific types of distress. All of these expressions of distress, however, require a comprehensive approach to help the child resolve them and to strengthen the abilities that lead to future confidence. The comprehensive

approach includes a number of the basic principles outlined in
Chapter One, all of which involve family relationships. In the
section that follows we will show how these principles can be
adapted to the grade-school years. Carrying out these principles enables children to use their distress to mobilize new skills
and to reaffirm old ones that have been lost. When these principles have been implemented for a reasonable period of time
and there is no progress being made, then a professional consultation should be sought. However, even if treatment is indicated, these basic principles should be continued.

## Floor Time for Grade-School Children

During this special unstructured time, about thirty minutes a
day at a minimum, you get down on the floor with your child,
trying to march to your child's drummer. Obviously, with an
older child, you might not literally be on the floor. You may be
sprawled on a couch or sitting side by side on the back steps,
taking a walk, or sweating it out on the basketball court. But the
goal, no matter where you are or what you are doing, is to follow your child's lead and tune in to whatever interests your
child. In other words, for those daily thirty minutes, your child
is the director—you're merely the assistant director. You follow
her lead in play or conversation, trying only to support and amplify her concerns.

The idea behind floor time is to build up a warm, trusting relationship in which shared attention, interaction, and communication are occurring on your child's terms. When that warm,
trusting relationship has begun to blossom, you're laying the
groundwork for tackling the particular distress or worries your
child may feel.

During the grade-school years, the child often doesn't de-
mand as much time and attention. On weekday evenings the
child may do her homework or watch TV while parents get
caught up on chores or work. On weekends there may be more

time for the family to be together but sometimes everyone may go their separate ways—dashing between soccer, camping, birthday parties, music lessons, housework, and errands.

Because of such packed schedules, family time needs to become all the more cherished and protected. For example, after dinner save the dishes for later and let the answering machine pick up calls. If one or both parents work long hours, they may need to make it a rule to be home from 6:00 to 8:30 P.M. for family time. After that, they can work at home or go back to the office if needed.

This is a tough concept for many busy working parents to implement. Some are so overworked and so rushed that they lose their sense of where their children may fit into their lives. Floor time is a way to regain that sense of connection with your children in ways that you may not have enjoyed since they were infants.

As a parent tunes into the interests of the slightly older child, sometimes it will involve pretending together, other times chitchat, and other times games. Your goal is to help your child express and enlarge upon whatever she has on her mind. This can be about school, friends, animals, Nintendo, or about Grandpa who just died—whatever the child's interests may be. If your child has constructed a castle and wants you to be the bad guy who attacks it, then play that role. If the child wants you to get down on all fours and bark like a dog, then do it. If she wants to talk about what a lousy parent you are because you didn't let her watch a certain show, then your job is to follow along on her theme.

"Tell me more about it," you might say. "Tell me the different ways I've messed up." If the child says, "My teacher is awful," don't say, "Don't talk about your teacher that way!" Instead you might say, "What did she do that was awful?"

The exchanges between the two of you needn't be deep or even relate to the events of the day. You are simply tuning in, being open to what the child wants to do or say, and becoming part of your child's world. The precise words you use aren't as important as the fact that you are, at least symbolically, down on the floor with your child. The spirit of floor time is what counts. The child needs the sense that parents can get on her level and stay interested in her.

Because all successful human relationships seem to have this kind of warm empathy at their core, my sense is that when children experience this feeling enough, they become more interested in understanding the needs of others. Also, through floor time you naturally mobilize and support all the developmental processes we have discussed throughout the book that are so vital to a child's sense of security, self-regulation, engagement with others, two-way communication, expression of emotional ideas, and logical thinking.

Floor time can have a very powerful effect. It gives a child a tremendous sense of being cared for, of feeling loved and secure, of being understood. It helps her feel that her parents are concerned about her as a person. It creates opportunities to make vague, private feelings—whether they are needy, scary, anxious, or angry ones—part of the world of ideas and relationships. In fact, it creates the whole basis for security, trust, and self-worth that a child will need from here on. It is hard to think of any childhood problem that is not at least partially helped through floor time.

As we've said, the rules of floor time are very simple: The child can't hurt you or break anything. Beyond that, the child is the complete and total boss. Your job is to follow along. You need not try to play psychiatrist and attempt to understand the unconscious elements of the child's play. You needn't interpret the child's feelings for her, saying, for example, "I can tell you were scared when you walked by those big kids." But as you spend more time together, you'll soon be able to read between the lines of your child's communications and pick up on certain emotional themes that she herself keeps coming back to.

Some children don't make it easy. What if your child says nothing? The key point to remember is that the child is always communicating—whether it be through words, posture, tone, gestures. Even her desire not to communicate is a communication. You can always make contact about something. Many parents make the mistake of taking their child too literally. If the child says, "I don't want to talk," parents respond to the words and give up, instead of asking, "Why don't you want to talk to me?" and then listening to the child's reasons. Or you could talk about why it's easier not to talk, and reflect on your own childhood when you didn't feel like talking. If you go with the flow and take what the child gives you, you can usually strike up a conversation on just about anything, including how boring she feels everything is. The trick is to avoid having a concrete agenda. Maybe you'll walk into your child's room, expecting a nice chat about school, friends, or a TV show, and she throws you a curve ball.

"Get out of my room! My homework is all done, so don't bug me any more!"

Don't be so tied to your plan that you say, "This is our time to talk!" Instead try observing, "Oh, you want me out of here," and then ask why it might be better if you were in the next room. Perhaps you two could talk about why she may be angry at you. Most kids are willing to talk for twenty minutes about what they don't like about their parents. Try to avoid getting turned off by the negative feelings. The more trouble your child has in hanging out with you, the more she needs that special time.

Floor time is harder for some parents than others. Some parents take to it intuitively, but most of us have difficulties shifting from the pace of the rest of our lives. Many parents want to be helpful to their child, but they find it hard just to relax and go through the simple process of listening and helping the child go in the direction she wants to go. Some of the pitfalls that we all fall into are getting bored, trying to control the theme, or not participating enough. That's because it is often difficult for many of us parents to be active and engaged without controlling the action. When we're not in charge, we start daydreaming.

Floor time can indeed be boring. A litany of baseball scores, or an endless lament over who was mean to whom in the third grade could drive any parent up the wall. But, as a general rule, you can usually get through your boredom if you watch for the types of themes that emerge from floor time. What is your child trying to tell you?

Sometimes bored feelings themselves are a mechanism that parents use to avoid seeing their child's real personality or real interests. For example, a parent may want a bold, assertive child and be reluctant to face the fact that his child is actually rather timid. Instead of tuning in to the reasons the child is timid and then helping the child feel more secure so that she begins to experiment with being assertive, the parent may simply tune out. If parents take this route they are actually contributing to the child's timidity through lack of involvement, which adds to the child's sense of uncertainty and her tendency to be passive.

Floor time is especially valuable for timid or insecure children, giving them, in effect, a second chance. Timidity itself does not mean a child cannot be creative and assertive once she becomes comfortable in a situation. But without an opportunity to garner confidence, a tendency to be passive and to avoid people and situations can compromise her abilities.

The first few weeks of floor time are rocky for many parents because they slip into a controlling mode. As a general rule, if you have clear expectations of what the child will say or do next, you are probably controlling the action too much. Floor time should be full of surprises, as your child takes off in entirely new directions. Ask yourself: "Am I asking too many questions? Am I telling my child what to do? When in doubt, listen more. The goal is to be a good listener and responder—

to be naturally curious and interested in your child. Floor time has a type of rhythm: When spending time with a good friend, you laugh, joke, listen to each other, and devote your full attention to each other. Floor time should be like that, not patronizing or contrived.

Some parents slip into the habit of merely watching their child's play instead of participating. That isn't floor time, even if the parent is just offering a commentary on what the child is doing but with his or her mind elsewhere. No genuine interaction is occurring.

To become more involved, the parent might say: "O.K. Do you want me to bring the train from the other direction?" You don't want to stay outside the drama, and you don't want to control the drama either. You want to be a part of the drama, so that your child has to interact with you and deal with you as a partner in play.

What if your child doesn't seem interested in having you participate. "No, I just want you to watch." So maybe you have a discussion about why you just have to watch. In doing so, you are engaging the child in an interaction with you. The child may say, "Shut up. I want to play with my soldiers." So you shut up for a while, watch the drama, and then say, "Can I do something now?" "No. You're still supposed to stay over here." "You mean I'm just the observer?" you may say. When you encourage the child to redefine your role, that becomes a drama within the drama.

If you have more than one child, you may need to reduce the amount of floor time for each. But I still urge you to try to carve out enough time for one-on-one sessions with each child. If you are available from after dinner until the children start getting ready for bed, there is usually enough time. But you can also be flexible. If you are home in the afternoons, you could do floor time then.

Once you get into the rhythm, you can incorporate floor time into car drives with your child or during each child's bath or into the bedtime ritual. You can spend twenty minutes or so chatting with each child while he or she gets undressed and ready for bed. Because a younger child's floor time usually will center on playing instead of talking, it's probably best to do floor time in an area where she has access to her toys and other play materials.

In two-parent families, floor time with several children is easier to arrange, of course. One parent can be with one child while the other spends time with the other child. Then you can alternate. Doing floor time is more challenging if you are a single parent. You can do group floor time—getting down on the floor and trying to tune in to each child. It's like leading an orchestra—and you may be playing three different themes. The same goes for teachers—there are many teachers out there who are terrific at floor time with groups of children.

With two (or more) children, you could designate one child as the "floor time leader" for the next half-hour. You march to that child's drummer, and you engineer it so that the other child or children are helpers in the drama. If she shakes her head no, then it's a perfect opening to discuss the reasons. After a half-hour (or later in the evening), the children can switch places.

This is the world of floor time. Whether it's with a five-year-old and her bears, a seven-year-old and his trains, or a nine-year-old who is talking about her gerbil or complaining about her soccer coach, you are marching to each child's drummer, following her or his lead and trying to help amplify, deepen, and thicken the plot in the particular drama being played out. As you can see, floor time is as much a philosophy of what children need as anything else. If you do floor time regularly, you'll probably find that during the rest of the day you'll be listening to your child more carefully and responding more thoughtfully. Over time you will also develop a warmer, closer relationship with your child—that I can promise. And the benefits—to the child's health, well-being, and overall emotional well-being—are incalculable.

## Problem-Solving with Grade-School Children

The idea behind problem-solving time is to help children to learn to be logical in their interactions and anticipate and solve challenges so that they can grow well intellectually and emotionally. Problem-solving time has some very separate goals from floor time. Unlike floor time, when you are following your child's lead, problem-solving time has more of a negotiated or shared agenda. You try to be respectful of what the child wants to talk about, but you have your own agenda as well. You might want to talk to the child about why she is so afraid of gym class. You might simply want to negotiate bedtime or how much time she has to spend on her homework. You can bring up subjects such as fighting with a sibling, rudeness, or schoolwork, "I see you got a D on that test. What happened?"

Problem-solving time is designed to help the two of you find out about specific challenges for your child. Then the two of you try to meet those challenges.

First you listen to your child's perspective and then you give your point of view. Remember you always have the prerogative of pulling rank. But understanding your child's viewpoint and giving her a chance to verbalize complaints, fears, or wishes can only be helpful. Don't assume you know what your child thinks and feels. And, even if you do, she needs to say it. Make sure that she, not you, does most of the talking.

Problem-solving need not have a special time. It can be done during dinner, in the car, at the shopping mall, or on the bus or subway as long as there is an opportunity to talk logically.

Sometimes it's hard to get started. Don't get discouraged. First, keep in mind that the child who doesn't talk very much may communicate with posture—sitting stiffly with arms crossed or shoulder and head slumped. You could comment on what you are observing. Or you could assume that the child has a good reason for not talking. Sometimes a child who says, "I can't remember" or "Nothing much happened" needs a little help or a little cueing. "Sometimes it's hard to remember all the stuff that goes on at school." Some children give you a little island of information and then stop and get perplexed again. So you'll need to cue them again.

Another obstacle to successful problem-solving sessions is that many children and parents talk past each other. They don't actually interact in a logical dialogue. (If you lecture your child, it is not a dialogue.) Some children come by this skill naturally; others have to learn it. The only way for a child to learn is through practice with adults and other children. Solving problems together creates an ideal opportunity. With the child who has problems with a consecutive dialogue, be happy with one or two direct responses and work up from there to five or six, then more. Eventually you'll be up to twenty or thirty. The first few exchanges are the hardest to close with a child who doesn't have an inclination to do so, because she is so used to getting distracted. For example, with a child who comes home from school looking upset, you may ask, "How was school?"

She ignores your query, opening the refrigerator. "What's on TV?"

Now comes the hard part, where you say, "I can tell you, but you didn't tell me how school was. Can we talk about that first?"

"What's for dinner?" she asks.

"I want to tell you what's for dinner," you say, persisting gently, "but you don't seem to want to answer my question."

"I don't want to answer your dumb questions!" she replies in exasperation.

Success! Even though she didn't give you the answer you were looking for, she did respond to your comments with comments of her own. She didn't go off on a tangent or ignore or tune out your words.

Keep in mind that with a child who is resistant, you may need to build up gradually. You don't want to turn a problem-solving session into a full-blown argument. About fifteen minutes is enough time to give your child the idea that there's something valuable to be learned here and to give her practice with it. (For children with auditory or other processing difficulties, a great deal more work may be needed in this area. I discuss this in *Playground Politics* and *The Child with Special Needs*.)

Many parents, especially those with a child who tends to be pensive or withdrawn, inadvertently allow problem-solving time to become a one-way street. They do most of the talking and miss opportunities to help their child take charge and be assertive. Many children require an extra second or two—or even five—to figure out their next step. But, accustomed to the natural rhythm of adult conversation, parents may move too quickly and take over. If the child is only saying yes or no all the time, it's your dialogue, and she isn't getting a chance to hone her skills for talking, thinking, and interacting.

Be careful not to get involved in a power struggle in which you are forcing the child to tell you everything. Help cue her and re-create the situation. Be supportive, but let her run with it once you help her begin a rhythm of sharing with you about what happened.

An added benefit of problem-solving time is that it does much more than just solve problems. Each discussion or negotiation helps the child practice her receptive and expressive language, as well as her logical thinking. Even if you have to pull rank, the process of negotiation is one of the best learning opportunities your child will ever have in logical thinking. And remember, the child who likes to talk the least needs to practice this skill the most.

Problem-solving time encourages negotiations. Let your child bargain. It's very helpful for children to have lawyer-to-lawyer dialogues with their parents about various issues. It's nine o'clock, and it's bedtime, and your child says, "Two more minutes of television!" You could pull rank and say, "No, you have to go to bed," grab her by the elbow, and guide her upstairs. Or you could decide to hear her argument.

"O.K. You've got thirty seconds to present your case," you could say.

That way, you get a good discussion going. You may make a small adjustment, or you may have to pull rank after ten minutes. The extra discussion time won't make the child feel that you're a softy when it comes to limits. Those kinds of logical exchanges help children become more comfortable with assertiveness and muscle-flexing, so that they are more able to use ideas instead of behavior, such as hitting or pushing, to get what they want.

While general problem-solving time will help in many situations, there are some situations that require using problem-solving time in a very distinct way. Some challenges are so formidable that you need to help your child prepare for them. When a child faces such a situation—teasing, speaking up in class, and so on—you can help by assisting your child in picturing the difficult situation; by anticipating her feelings; by picturing what she routinely does in those situations; and then by picturing alternative ways to meet her needs. This is a very effective way for children (and adults) to build a feeling of security and confidence in situations that are formidable or frightening.

It is tempting to lecture on alternatives instead of helping the child picture the situation, her feelings, her routine behavior, and the alternatives. This is not helpful. A child who can anticipate a situation herself is no longer the victim of her own behavior. Most of us fall into patterns; we do things reflexively. Anticipating the challenging situation and our feelings in that situation provides perspective. Insecurity and fears about how to cope with new people, what to do in class, or any scary situation can be reduced in this way.

As we've seen, problem-solving time is an opportunity for children to practice logical thinking and to learn to cope with difficult challenges and fear and anxiety. In situations of illness, divorce, moving, or other big challenges, it can be especially helpful.

## Empathizing with the Child's Point of View

To understand a child, you must first be able to empathize with her goals, no matter what they are. If you try to listen and learn why your child is behaving the way she is, how her actions fit into her overall view of the world, it's a lot easier to begin working on changing her behavior. Children have good reasons for doing what they do. Whether or not we agree with them, parents need to understand what those reasons are before we can ever hope to change a child's behavior. (Sometimes, once we understand our child's reasons for doing things, we may not want to change them at all.)

The third principle uses the logical dialogue that you've begun with your child to help you empathize with your child, no matter what situation you are discussing and no matter what challenges your child faces at the moment. Each child's coping strategy is minimizing some pain of the moment. And no matter how silly or nonsensical parents think the behavior is, we need to show respect when learning from the child her reason for doing it that way.

If your child, for instance, is acting up in class, or if she wants to hit a sibling, ask yourself, "Can I figure out why she sees the world this way? What's in it for her?"

Empathizing with, rather than criticizing, some of the child's feelings can be difficult for parents—not because we don't want to but ironically because parents care about the child so much. Many parents find it difficult, for example, to handle feelings like rejection, humiliation, and embarrassment in their child. When a child complains of these feelings, they may comment, "You shouldn't feel that way. Of course Alec likes you" or, "Oh, everyone makes mistakes in class. There's no need to feel embarrassed."

When we hear these feelings we tend to be hard on ourselves. If you were a better father or mother, your child wouldn't suffer this way. But all feelings are part of the human drama. The bad feelings come along with the good feelings—love, pride, joy, happiness—and their presence in a child does not diminish us as parents.

Empathy does not mean agreeing. But before you disagree, you want to understand the child's perspective. You want to understand the child's feelings surrounding the problem behaviors. That doesn't mean playing psychiatrist. Far from it. A lot of parents assume that if they don't know the underlying reasons behind their child's behavior, then there is nothing they can do about it. But if you simply recognize and empathize with the feelings, it often helps a child enormously. You are not in an adversarial position but instead more like a good friend who is saying, "So that's how you feel sometimes?"

When you last were upset or had a problem, what helped more than having your spouse or a friend listen patiently and sympathetically while you elaborated your pain and anguish? This gave you a chance to better understand the main issues at stake; what the problem was really about, what part you played, what solutions there might be. With warmth and support, problems become both clearer and more tolerable. This applies to children as well.

For instance, say a child is furious at not being allowed to play video games. By empathizing, Mom gets a chance to understand where the child is coming from. In the end, she may decide that the child is unreasonable and that she needs to do her homework. But having reached that conclusion by empathizing with her child rather than reacting defensively, she'll feel more comfortable saying no. She is less likely to worry that she is being mean; the child will feel that the mother's behavior is is not arbitrary. Empathizing doesn't mean giving in to your child; it just means listening without getting defensive.

An important part of this step of empathizing with your child is to identify the child's underlying assumptions. People have feelings based on underlying assumptions of how the world works. Your goal is to figure these out. Does the child assume,

"I run the world here. I'm the boss"? Or perhaps your child assumes that if she argues with her friends, they will leave her. Or perhaps she assumes that, if she challenges you or moves out from under your wing, she'll lose your love and support.

These underlying assumptions can be tough to get at. But regular floor time and problem-solving sessions will make it a lot easier. And once you think you've figured it out, play it back to the child. If you are right, she will feel understood and that you have listened. If not, you can avoid misunderstanding and keep exploring the child's point of view.

The goal here is to help the child solve the problem at hand—such as curbing aggression or feeling less worried—but to do so in a framework that meets the child's own objectives. For example, the goals might be to be close to certain friends, to get more attention from her parents or a teacher, or to get her own way. In other words, often we can help the child have her cake and eat it too. By empathizing with the child's perspective we often can help her find ways to meet her own needs that don't cause her even more trouble at home or at school.

### Breaking Grade School Challenges into Small Pieces

One way to encourage your child to tackle a hard problem or challenge is by constantly giving her little successes to feel good about. By helping your child put one toe at a time into the water (instead of having to plunge in headfirst), you meet the child's need to feel satisfied with herself, avoiding a feeling of hopelessness. "What's the use? I'm never going to be any good at math (or soccer)! No one is going to like me." The goal here is to break down any particular challenge so that the child can have a sense of success as she masters one step at a time.

Take another common school problem—a child is having difficulties with math. As we have seen, children who have trouble with math often have trouble picturing quantity. They don't have a way of intuitively knowing that ten is twice as big as five, or that twenty is twice as big as ten. If you just try to make a child memorize better, she will feel like a failure. And if you jump in too quickly, the child may feel that you're trying to make her feel bad—not because you are, but because math has always aroused these feelings in her.

To start, you might instead help the child stack blocks up, so that she can see the difference between ten blocks and five blocks. As a second step you could have her show with her hands (and her imagination) what ten blocks and five blocks look like. Then, as a third step, you could begin with very easy numbers, such as $1 + 1 = 2$ and $2 + 2 = 4$, making sure that she always first pictures the quantities in her head. By helping your child succeed in these small steps, you meet her need for self-satisfaction while avoiding self-defeat.

With ingenuity the principle works on just about any fears and hurdles that might face a child. Perhaps she gets panicky about performing in front of a large group. You can suggest that she first perform for the family and then for a few friends before she has to venture onstage in a big auditorium. Or perhaps a child is unusually timid about going to a friend's house to play. The child could begin by inviting that friend over several times, or perhaps visiting the other house with a parent. A child who is afraid of dogs or cats might be introduced to a particularly friendly one a bit at a time. All sorts of fears—bedtime fears, school phobias, fears about crowds, or fear of riding a bike—can be approached in this way.

Often there are multiple challenges, such as a child who likes to have her own way, who is afraid of the dark, who hits her sister, and who won't get on the school bus. Where do you start? Well, not on all fronts! Instead you could pick out one or two things, such as not physically hurting other people, feeling safe at night, or getting on the bus without a struggle. Then you break that challenge down, say not hitting her sister for a whole afternoon, or leaving the door open from her darkened room to the hall, or riding other buses with you. Only when there is some success with that one goal do you move on to the next. That way, the child will have some short-term satisfaction and confidence in herself that will motivate her to keep going.

## Setting Limits for Grade-School-Age Children

Limits are as important as empathy and encouragement. They give children security and guidance. Limit-setting works best when combined with extra floor time. That way, you assuage any guilt you may feel about having to set the limits in the first place (especially when you've basically got a good kid), and you keep nurturing your relationship with your children so that they'll abide by the limits. If your children are to feel good about themselves and safe in the world, they need limits as well as empathy, guidance, and love.

In deciding what to limit, it's best to pick a single area, set the boundaries wide, and then firmly enforce them. In other words, it is better to use one's energy to win one battle than to get worn out in lots of little ones. Take one key issue at a time. As we said before, don't try to wage a war on several fronts at once, or set very narrow, strict rules.

Methods of punishment should never be cold and arbitrary. They must always be surrounded by an empathetic, respectful relationship. Negotiate what the punishments and rewards will be ahead of time. There shouldn't be any surprises, and justice should be impartial. But keep in mind what Henry Kissinger said about international relations: "The other side has to pay a price that they feel is too high." Consider limiting TV or computer games, setting an earlier bedtime, KP duty, or canceling an outing. Each child is different: for some, a day without computer games is a major punishment; for others, it may take a week of no TV. To be effective, the punishment must be meaningful so that it challenges the child to do better in the future.

Some parents are uncomfortable with the use of food, such as withholding desserts as a punishment, fearing that it could lead to eating disorders. Actually, as long as your family's attitudes about food, hunger, and other bodily functions are flexible and not rigid, it's perfectly fine to make certain foods a special treat that can be withheld as part of limit-setting. But recognize that this will have the effect of making the dessert or sweet more desirable. All sanctions should be comfortable within your own family value system.

Try to make sure your limits are clear and automatic and that you can stick to them. Avoid half-hearted, spur-of-the-moment limit-setting that ends with somebody yelling or criticizing. When you and your child have set up limits well in advance and have debated them enough, you're less likely to get frazzled and overwhelmed when you're trying to implement them.

If you're doing enough floor time with your child, you'll be able to set more effective limits when they're needed. Your goals in setting limits are to teach greater empathy and respect for others. By combining empathy with setting limits you are setting an example of such behavior.

When a child knows the limits in advance and knows that her parents will stick to them, the parents can actually empathize with the child's plight while, at the same time, creating a firm sense of structure. The goal is to be iron tough in setting limits and enforcing them yet be empathetic to the child's plight of having to pay the price. By helping the child with your anticipatory discussions, she is less likely to dig a hole for herself. The automatic pre-discussed sanctions allow you to take an empathic, helpful stance.

Even a basically obedient child probably has her "hand in the cookie jar" somewhere and needs some limits set. Every child can benefit from some limits applied to real situations. Even the child who appears not to need limits needs to practice bumping against authority figures somewhere in life—and better now than in college or in the workplace.

Fear of a child's discomfort or anger, especially with a grade-school or older child, is a major reason why limits are hard for some parents. When two parents support one another, this can be much easier. Also, by combining time together to solve particular problems and extra empathy with the limits, you can avoid setting up a power struggle.

Imposing your will through sheer force will prove to be counterproductive. The more angry you and your child become, the more closeness and empathy will be needed. It's not easy: We all get trapped in our angry feelings, and we have a tendency to want to push away from the situation or the person who is angering us. So you'll have to go against the grain. Keep in mind that children can generally shift gears more easily than parents can. They forgive more quickly than adults if they have had the chance to grow up basically secure and trusting.

Power struggles with your child can be infuriating because adults hate to lose face. But intimidating and humiliating your child will never lead to self-discipline. The child will only want to protect herself and get around you next time. Instead, helping a child save face and feel self-respect while following your guidance lets her associate cooperation with feelings of positive self-esteem.

Some parents are more predisposed to being empathetic and playful and may find it harder to set any limits at all. But children require both loving attention and limits, particularly when the challenges are difficult. When increasing both limits and relating together, you are giving more and expecting more.

The five principles outlined here are meant not to be a rigid agenda but to set a general approach and philosophy of what children need. I hope that, over time, these five steps can become a part of family life. When they do, they establish a warm, predictable, structured base for a child. Even with the demands of work and school, you automatically find yourself taking that half-hour or more a day for one-on-one time with your child. That child becomes comfortable bringing home the disappointments and problems of the school day, because you listen and empathize rather than simply imposing your will. You ask for manageable tasks to be carried out and watch for hurdles that might appear overwhelming. Finally, you set firm limits that you stick to while continuing the warm communication that has become habitual. In a home run along these principles a child can gather strength and skills to confront the changing opportunities and challenges of the larger world.

# 5

........

# The Secure and
# Confident Adolescent

As CHILDREN GROW INTO ADOLESCENCE, THEY DEVELOP
additional abilities that enable them to feel secure. With these
same abilities, however, they also open themselves up to new
types of insecurity. Their degree of mastery of these abilities
and the basic ones laid down earlier in their lives will determine
how secure they can become.

## New Strengths in Adolescence

The internal standard we talked about in the last chapter, the
inner yardstick by which to evaluate new experience, is the
foundation for future stability. From late childhood on, the
child is becoming able to live in two worlds: the world inside
himself and the world of daily experience.

### Growing Sense of Self

A growing sense of self allows the adolescent to put new experiences in context. This is what judgment is all about. Judgment draws upon the accumulation of wisdom developed over

time. So many of the temptations facing the adolescent require good judgment—drugs or alcohol; risk-taking behavior; new opportunities to explore sexuality. In addition, there are decisions to be made about the future: education beyond high school; career planning; new relationships; involvement in the community and beyond; participation in music, sports, and other activities.

The adolescent's world is expanding dramatically in a variety of new areas. At the same time, there is a major metamorphosis from the body of a child to the body of an almost-adult with defined sexual characteristics. The adult world that has always seemed in the far-distant future is now, in part, here. Adolescence is a long transition, but within it are dramatic physical, emotional, intellectual, and social changes. The key challenge for the adolescent is to keep developing internal standards and a sense of self from which he can embrace an ever-broadening range of changes in his own body, new interests, intellectual skills, and new social worlds. Eventually, he will need to maintain his growing sense of self and inner standards more and more on his own as he moves from his family into advanced education, work, or both.

## Anticipating the Future

Adolescents can now think in terms of the long-term future, hypothetically and probabilistically. They can picture a world of peace where people are helping one another. They can also picture a world at war where people are destroying one another. Against this background, they are considering their own plans. They can picture different careers for themselves and can begin thinking in terms of the likelihood of one of these outcomes versus another. How likely is it that they will become a concert pianist? How likely is it that they will become a major-league baseball player? How likely is it that they will go to college, get a good job, and meet somebody that they can love and marry? Will the economy support their career interests? Will the political situation allow them to pursue their goals? These are all concerns that go through the minds of adolescents, more or less, depending on their age and on the particular person.

Many adolescents are also aware of the fact that much of the burden for coping with the problems of the future and leading the world will fall in their hands and in the hands of those younger than they. This ushers adolescents into a wider reality, one that they were protected from in the past. To be sure, in other countries there are adolescents who are already facing responsibility and danger—we see adolescents supporting their families, serving in the military, or in active political movements. Many in the United States were involved in political action during the Vietnam War. But for the most part, in recent history (since World War II) adolescents in developing nations have enjoyed the luxury of being able to take their time in the transition from childhood to adulthood. The realities they need to confront for the future are more personal ones, having to do with school and work and relationships. However, events such as violence in cities, epidemics, or terrorist attacks can thrust adolescents, like all of us, into the uncertainties of the larger world.

In this way, the ability to think about the future becomes a new responsibility. Adolescents can consider how best to create a safe and secure world. Some adolescents will retreat from this challenge or show various signs of distress that we will discuss shortly. Others will be able to embrace this new awareness and grow from it.

## Dealing with Dependency

One of the first issues that a child confronts in adolescence is the issue of his own dependency, vulnerability, or neediness. Years ago, Peter Blos, a psychoanalytic pioneer studying adolescence, pointed out that to feel strong and independent, the adolescent must come to grips with all his earlier longings. The desire to be cared for and nurtured may be felt even more strongly in the face of all the physical changes and all the new opportunities. How does the child who wants more of his mother's warmth manage to act strong and independent and at the same time stay clear of his parents? It's a hard dilemma for the teenager, and different individuals deal with it in very different ways. Some establish a pseudo-independence. They posture and walk around denying and criticizing their parents a great deal. That's one way of coping with that strong yearning for more "chicken soup" from their parents. Some get very angry. Others act out in different ways.

Thus, one of the key challenges for parents at this time is to sneak in the nurturing without embarrassing the teenager. How do you accomplish this? You sneak it in when you are driving your child to a friend's house; when you are hanging out with your child at dinner; and in activities you do together. Join your teenager in his activities (sports, music, a hike). "Floor time" becomes even more important in adolescence, but it's not on the floor anymore—it's in the car, shooting baskets, taking a walk, looking through magazines. It's schmoozing about school, accepting the child's complaints about yourself and about teachers and adults in general. Adolescents will accept your caring concern on their terms (for example, if you are driving them somewhere they want to go or listening to their opinions or talking about what they're interested in). Keep hanging out and tuning in to where they are. Otherwise, they won't accept the nurturing well and it could lead to conflict.

The importance of providing increased support and security at this time is illustrated by the problems faced by children who grow up without many of these basic emotional needs being met. Adolescents from deprived backgrounds or from dysfunctional families, or with families that are just too busy, often don't get their dependency needs met in the early years. This is compounded by the pressures to become more independent in adolescence. To prevent such children from turning into antisocial adults requires special help. Milt Shore, a psychologist and colleague, ran a program for such children many years ago in Boston. The moment children dropped out of school, a mentor was brought in. The mentor was a very skilled, streetwise psychologist who taught the kids math at a gas station as they were trying to hold down a job. He taught them about love by being at the police station when they got into trouble. He was a twenty-four-hour kind of mentor. For a couple of years, he combined academics with emotional and social support in an exceptional way and provided what was missing to these acting-out, defiant, angry teenagers.

More than twenty years later there is follow-up data on these children. Eighty percent of the kids in the program are doing reasonably well. They're not in the criminal justice system and not in the mental health system, they're working, and they have families. Eighty percent of the kids who were identified as being similarly at risk but who didn't participate in this mentoring program are either in the criminal justice system or in the mental health system with severe difficulties. This program shows that there can be dramatic change, even when help is offered at later ages to children with significant challenges. It's not too late, even in the teen years.

For the child in a basically supportive family, the task is much easier. Nevertheless, many parents tend to get so busy with other things or so discouraged by their teenagers' negativism that they do not persist in "slipping in" that extra nurturance. Because of children's need for respect and their sensitivity to humiliation (because they as yet are unsure of their own self respect), it is critical to make sure that the nurturance is done on the children's turf in terms of their own interests. It's not an easy thing for parents to do, along with trying to guide, educate, and instill values. This effort requires great empathy.

## Mastering Sexuality

Hormonal changes and secondary sex characteristics are now emerging. This affects the child at a biological level, because the hormonal changes will affect mood directly, and at a psychological level as well, because physical and mood changes alter the perceptions a person has about his body. Does he welcome the changes, or is he scared about them? Will he act on his sexual impulses or be cautious?

In early adolescence, there are also changes in eating habits, concepts of beauty or handsomeness, and body-image changes. Children experiment with their image (for example, blue spiked hair, tattoos, and other body adornments).

Those of us who grew up in the fifties and sixties thought that nothing more could shock us. But as a parent seeing kids with hair shaved down the middle, or with nose or navel rings, I was surprised. Every generation seems to find a way to exaggerate body changes in a way that will startle the prior generation.

Parents' worries about sexuality have intensified in recent years. Not only is there is great concern about children at ages twelve or thirteen beginning to act out sexually, there is new awareness of sexually transmitted diseases, including the life-threatening risk of AIDS.

As parents, we can react to children's sexuality and body concerns with different attitudes. We can see their behavior as a manifestation of some uncertainty about the body and of trying to cope with its changes through exaggeration, avoidance, or inhibition. Or we can interpret the child's behavior as provocative. If we get on the latter tangent and engage in arguments all the time about tattoos or earrings or this or that kind of hairstyle or clothing, this creates a continuing power struggle that interferes with the dependency, nurturing, and respect the child needs. In such a situation, the child's anxiety about body changes will only increase, along with the need for exaggerated behavior. Children require some guidance regarding what's medically healthy, on the one hand, and what's a reasonable expression, on the other hand. The underlying anxiety in your tone of voice, your acceptance of the child's thinking, and your reasoning together about what can be done will be useful to adolescents as they work out some of their anxieties about their bodies.

Schools, not just families, get involved in these issues. Some schools take a very hard line on dress codes and uniforms. Adolescents who like to wear tops that show a bit of midriff or baggy jeans see school prohibitions as a violation of their freedom of expression. Both parents and schools need to find ways to strike a balance between that freedom and the need to feel safe, secure, and accepted.

Sexuality and body-image concerns are issues that persist throughout one's life. Adolescents who can develop pictures of themselves and their bodies that are consistent with reality and an emerging "inner standard" will get this process off to a good start. This inner standard will reflect family relationships and values. If these relationships are nurturing and supportive, while promoting a reasonable degree of individual expression, they will provide the guidance teenagers need.

## Mastering Aggression

As children become bigger and stronger, the need to control aggression takes on greater importance. Adolescents experiment with aggression in different ways—some through sports and organized activities, some through fighting, some through stealing, some even through using weapons such as guns and knives. Dangerous aggression has its roots in earlier childhood. If the child has been deprived of consistent care and constructive limits early in life (for example, if there have been many foster care placements, unstable adults in the house, addicted parents or a history of abuse), the likelihood of dangerous aggression is much higher. Even in middle-income and wealthy families, changing nannies or rotating daycare staffs can result in inconsistent early nurturing and multiple experiences of loss.

Certain kinds of personalities are also more likely to have problems with aggression. An underreactive, stimulus-craving child—one who craves a lot of sensory input, tends to be insensitive to pain, and is somewhat fearless—often copes with anxiety through activity and aggression. But with a lot of nurturance, good limits, and practice in regulating his activity level, he may channel that aggression. Such a child might become an energetic entrepreneur, a surgeon, a mountain climber, or an athlete. If he learns to care about other people and have true empathy, he can adapt that activity to work that serves his family and society.

On the other hand, if such a child does not have nurturing care and constructive limits, he may feel no real connection to the human race, treating people as "things." If that child deals with his frustrations and insecurities with increased sensory-seeking activity and aggression, there is a higher likelihood of destructive behavior and illegal activity when the child reaches adolescence.

One can see these negative tendencies emerging in a certain percentage of teenagers in all societal groups, but particularly among the poor. Society has two choices: Build more prisons, or support special programs in the schools and communities, including mentoring. (My earlier book, Growth of the Mind, has a detailed discussion of such programs.)

In adolescence, however, there is often a psychological "second chance." We can take advantage of this phenomenon by increasing support (through such efforts as mentoring relationships), setting firm limits in a respectful way, providing better one-on-one and small-group education and job training, and getting these teenagers involved in activities that channel aggression (sports, dance, music). Kids who are gifted enough athletically often get these experiences from their coaches. Academically gifted children often get special support from teachers. But these experiences are needed by all adolescents, not just the very gifted.

## Ability to Delay Gratification

Adolescents are moving from living in the here and now to recognizing that they have a past and a future. By mid-adolescence, kids are becoming aware of how what has happened in the past influences the present. They're also beginning to think about what they're going to do after high school. They're expanding their interests in terms of their current peer group into the community they're living in. Some get concerned with politics. Others get concerned with environmental issues. Many develop an interest in living abroad or learning about other cultures.

This growing awareness can lead to a sense of responsibility. Some kids now study harder so they can go to a good college and have a good career. Children who feel more secure have something to look forward to. They use their cognitive skills to anticipate the future and explore broader interests. Now a teenager can anticipate many possible futures through formulating different possibilities.

Children who are anxious and stressed, however, live more in the here and now. They move back into the concrete, day-to-day, moment-to-moment existence of the grade-school years. Children who are in a lot of emotional turmoil can't think ahead easily. They are too anxious about the here and now. When asked, "Why did you do that?" these children say, "Because it felt good [at the moment]."

## Greater Ability to Learn

Adolescents are increasingly able to process what they see and hear into their own patterns and images. They are able to remember, organize, and comprehend what they hear and read, to create new verbal images and stories, and to consider many different alternatives for the future. Some have learning challenges or disabilities. They may have auditory processing or visual/spatial-processing problems, or a general problem with sequencing actions and information. Children who forget to hand in their homework or forget they had an appointment may be showing evidence of sequencing problems.

Adolescents with these processing problems may be more "all-or-nothing" thinkers. If they have unresolved issues around dependency, limit-setting, sexuality, and aggression, there is now a double problem. On the one hand, parents and teachers must work on these processing challenges. For example, they can help children visualize their world and picture what's going to happen tomorrow as well as what just happened today. Having a picture in mind can improve the ability to plan and sequence. Practice at anticipating challenging emotional and social situations (picturing them ahead of time) and working out solutions in advance is highly useful. At the same time, the five principles we describe at the end of the chapter will help the adolescent feel more secure and deal with the continuing problems around dependency, limits, or aggression.

## Intimacy

The ability to form intimate relationships becomes crucially important during adolescence. Hanging out in a group or one-on-one, teenagers seek closer friendships. Obviously the ability to engage others in this way builds on earlier family experiences with intimacy.

Many parents report today that kids are hanging out in groups well up into their twenties. There is less one-on-one dating. Even though there's more emphasis on sexuality and more sexual acting out, many kids avoid too much intimacy, and their main relationships are with the group—often a combined boy and girl group. As a college psychology major and friend of my oldest daughter told me, "I don't need to date. I have enough pleasure hanging out in the group. But on the other hand, it's not so good because there's no motivation to date. I never feel lonely."

Exploring relationships through group dynamics may be very useful for many teenagers. One-on-one intimacy is challenging and requires all the emotional and reflective thinking capacities we have been describing. In unsettled times, when there are worries about the dangers of sexual activity or about the future, it may take longer for teenagers to develop stable, one-on-one relationships.

Intimacy also involves a gradual shift from dependency on one's family relationships to carrying standards, judgment, confidence, and the ability to care for others "inside" and forming stable, intimate relationships outside the family. This is a gradual process with many ebbs and flows.

As indicated earlier, adolescence requires young adults to be more involved in the concerns of the world. In order to do this, they will need to empathize with and understand a range of individuals from other cultures, people with decidedly different backgrounds. In other words, they will have to broaden their sense of humanity from the narrow, protected world of childhood. This will mean understanding those with whom one is in conflict as well as those with whom one is likely to collaborate.

Some adolescents tend to form very narrow, rigid identities, whereas others form more broad-based identities that can incorporate an understanding of others. These days, in particular, adolescents will be required to broaden their sense of empathy and therefore, to some degree, their own identities. They will also need to overcome tendencies toward stereotyping others and will have to master higher levels of reflective thinking. That makes negotiation and cooperation possible.

A range of competencies are thus part of our definition of the secure adolescent. It includes all the traditional ones that we've known about for some time—a growing sense of self and more sophisticated judgment as well as a broadening of identity to include new peer, school, work, and romantic interests. However, this process also involves, as we have been describing, an increasingly urgent challenge—the skills and imagination to participate in the creation of safety and security for the future.

## Signs of Distress in Adolescents

Adolescents can have many of the same signs of insecurity as school-age children, but the former can also show additional signs of distress due to the increased responsibilities of adolescence. We may, for example, see more difficulty with school work and sexual identity, as well as increasing rebellious behavior. Because adolescents are now concerned about their long-term future, their anxieties will extend beyond the immediate. A sense of angst can develop, for some, into despair and depression. Helping adolescents to overcome and deal with such anxieties and to solve problems with constructive solutions will require a combined family, community, and national effort.

The following sections describe signs of insecurity and anxiety a parent can watch for and ways of helping with each particular problem. The next section outlines more general principles of increasing security in adolescence.

### Lack of Age-Expected Relationships and Interests

Adolescents are typically expanding their range of activities to involve new hobbies, different subjects at school, music, sports, and the like. A teenager who seems to avoid the interests and activities that are typical for most adolescents may have underlying worries about his future. While teenagers vary in the breadth of their interests, a lack of new interests at this age is a cause for concern. Most teenagers will find an interest in a particular school subject, or in after school activities involving music, sports, dance, chess club, math club, computers, or other skills and passions.

Even more noticeable, however, will be the child who is not developing the age-expected expansion in his or her relationships. As we mentioned, in adolescence there is greater intimacy, a closer network, and often a deeper sense of involvement with a few cherished friends. There is sexual interest by mid- to late adolescence, as well as relationships forming with adults, such as a teacher or coach. Often, there can be a more mature involvement with extended family, such as grandparents, even with helping to care for grandparents who may require some assistance. All of these are part of the age-expected broadening of a range of interests and relationships. When this is not occurring and a child is hiding away playing computer games or watching TV for hours and hours, this can be a sign of underlying distress.

If the child is doing O.K. at school and getting his work done, it can be easy to miss the fact that he may be suffering. The concern here is not just simply the child who is taking a little more time to develop some of the typical interests of adolescents; this happens all the time. Teenagers vary, for example, in how soon they develop sexual interests—some not until the very end of adolescence, others very early in adolescence. The key is to look at whether a child is gradually moving into these areas and beginning to show some general signs of interest. It may start with a child taking more care in his own dress; this in itself can be a sign of a growing interest in being more grown up and of a budding interest in sexuality. It may start with discussions about relatives who are doing interesting work without necessarily talking about his own possible career interests. But if one doesn't see these or other signs of broadening enthusiasm, it may be a sign of worry about growing up.

Often, children who are retreating from age-expected relationships are very apathetic and listless and seem passive. Some will be quite depressed underneath their seemingly apathetic and disinterested exterior.

In such circumstances, it's particularly important to offer consistent warm support as part of an ongoing nurturing relationship. This will help the teenager broaden his interest in relationships. Often, by first working on the family relationships, the adolescent will become more comfortable reaching out.

## Obsessive Interests

Many of the interests of adolescents will appear idiosyncratic or unusual to parents. There may be seemingly bizarre tastes in music or clothing, particular actors or actresses, or very different political beliefs. In and of themselves, this is part of the exploration and individuality of adolescents (and all people).

It can be a sign of distress, however, when the unusual interest dominates all other areas of the child's life. If there are no longer other interests in peer relationships, school activities, academic work, and family life, a parent might be concerned. For example, sometimes teenagers become involved in a particular set of activities, sometimes cult-related, that alter the way they dress, their friendship patterns, their attention to school work, and their openness and closeness with their family. In such cases, parents should take note, staying open and attentive and spending more time together so as to get a handle on what may be going on. It is easy to underestimate the value of just hanging out with a teenager, or staying available even in the face of rebuffs and silence.

## Preoccupation with One's Own Body

Family attitudes toward food, exercise, and body types play a role here, too, as do media representations of "ideal" physiques. As we saw, during adolescence a child may have a variety of preoccupations with his or her own body, including the typical ones having to do with how attractive he or she is. However, if these are excessive or overwhelmingly intense (for example, a child won't go to activities because he or she has acne), the adolescent needs help and support. Adolescents are prone to become very preoccupied with issues of eating and weight control. This, too, may interfere with other activities, requiring professional attention when it begins to reach dominating proportions in the child's life. It is important to distinguish whether it is a normal concern or a sign of anxiety and distress.

### Precocious or Overinvolvement in Sexual Behavior

Many adolescents begin experimenting with sexual behavior in a risky manner even during early adolescence. This can become a preoccupation, dominating more and more of adolescents' lives as they look for this or that partner. However, an excessive and precocious investment in sexual activity can be a sign of distress and signal deeper concerns. If the individual is seeking security through a relationship that he can't find elsewhere—or trying to work out feelings about his own body or about family conflicts—it's important to see this as a possible sign of distress and offer assistance.

### Risk-Taking Behavior

Adolescents can engage in many risk-taking behaviors, from driving over the speed limit to driving while intoxicated to breaking the law through shoplifting, for example. Though risk-taking behavior appears to be a facet of adolescence, it can become part of a pattern of danger; it is very important to deal with this undesirable behavior quickly. It signals possible distress and problems with self-discipline and self-regulation.

## Alcohol and Drugs

Many adolescents develop a reliance on illegal drugs as a way of stabilizing their moods or becoming comfortable socially. They also may try to experiment with altered mental states. All of these require immediate attention and a comprehensive treatment program.

Similarly, many teenagers use alcohol for the same reasons as well as to experiment with risk-taking. Teenagers will vary in how often and how much they drink. Parents need to be aware of their teenager's behavior and patterns so that they can determine what type of help is needed.

## Fears, Worries, and Anxieties

Like grade-school children, adolescents may experience a great deal of fear, worry, and anxiety. It can show itself with nightmares, being frightened of going out of the house during the day, or feelings of internal anxiety. Or there may be chronic feelings of apprehensiveness and vigilance.

Often, during adolescence, anxiety can be displaced onto other matters. An adolescent, for example, may be anxious about global warming and about the uncertainty of the future, but may put that anxiety into a fear that he will or won't get into a particular college or a fear about not getting a job. In other words, a general feeling of insecurity may come out around issues that are a little less frightening than one's own survival. Certainly, one might feel insecure if one doesn't have a job or doesn't get accepted to a college, but those pale in comparison to the insecurity of fearing that one's own survival is in jeopardy. One must not always assume that the way in which an adolescent expresses his worries or anxieties necessarily relates to his true underlying concern. Often, anxiety about family problems will be expressed through worries about school or friendships.

Therefore, it is always important, as with other signs of distress, to maintain a communication process in which the child feels secure and nurtured, and can begin expressing his feelings more fully. These issues can then begin to emerge.

## Sadness and Depression

There are many reasons adolescents will feel sad or demoralized when involved in many new interests and activities; a relationship that isn't going in the "right" direction, messing up on an exam, and a power struggle with a parent or teacher are common examples. Depression, however, is different, taking a different form in the adolescent than it does in the grade-school child. While the grade-school child may be depressed about something immediate in his world—being rejected by a peer, parents paying more attention to a younger sibling, or anger at a parent for being unavailable—an adolescent will internalize more of his feelings and will be more likely to feel worthless or like a bad person, even hopeless and helpless about the future. Because the adolescent has a more internalized sense of self and can consider hypothetical possibilities and probabilities, he is able to have a deeper internal dialogue with himself. When his mood is depressed, he can have many more self-accusatory and negative feelings. There is even a risk with adolescents of trying to escape these feelings by using drugs and alcohol or engaging in risk-taking behavior like driving fast. There is also the risk of suicidal behaviors. Depression can also lead to acting out aggressively and hurting others in what may primarily be a self-destructive act.

It is, therefore, important to identify sadness and depression in adolescents as early as possible and to form the long nurturing relationships that will allow the depth of the sadness to emerge. If this continues or deepens into depression, it is vital to seek professional consultation.

*Fear of the Future*

Fear of the future is a concern for many adolescents. It may focus on their prospects for work, college, future relationships, or having a family of their own. These common fears can be deepened by fear regarding the world's safety and future survival. Adolescents are especially vulnerable to feeling insecure and uncertain because of all the changes they are going through and the uncertainties they are facing as they get ready for adulthood.

In adolescence, therefore, the uncertainty about themselves or the world surviving is no longer only a catastrophic fantasy. Because adolescents can understand the gravity of such problems as terrorist attacks, environmental pollution, and nuclear proliferation, their worries cannot be dismissed as fantasy or with easy reassurance. Fear of the future, however, is often founded on global concerns as well as personal ones. It can be hard to disentangle where the real concerns are. For some it may be the fear of separating from family or going off to college, for others it may be a sense that war or disaster may threaten their world, and for many it will be both.

Here, too, the best way to get a handle on these concerns is to continue a close, respectful relationship with an adolescent, avoiding unnecessary criticism or conflict over small rebellions. This will help disentangle where the anxieties lie and help the adolescent put his fear of the future into perspective. Typically, when adolescents or adults, or younger children for that matter, are anxious and worried, they will tend to exaggerate a worry because their thinking becomes less reflective than it otherwise would be. We all tend to slip into all-or-nothing thinking at times of acute anxiety. Adolescents who can assess probabilities can look at the likelihood of bad or good things happening and will be better able to evaluate the worry. Generally, they will see that the chances are likely that they will be safe and secure, at least for the short-term future, once their anxiety has calmed down. Also, helping them participate in discussions of policy or in organizations working toward conflict resolution or environmental protection will help them feel that they are doing something to help rather than being a passive, helpless bystander.

## Helping Adolescents Become More Secure

The signs of distress discussed above can be used as a window of opportunity to help adolescents master new strengths and inner confidence. To do this, there are three overriding principles.

1. *Slip in the nurturing.* You need to keep this going, even though your child is now a teenager and says he doesn't need it. As we mentioned earlier, while you have to provide that "chicken soup," you also have to do it with a lot of respect for the child's autonomy, emerging independence, and strength. The one key complaint from teenagers, boys and girls alike, is "My parents don't respect me." Then the parents say, "Well, there's nothing to respect. He's messing up at school." As one child who has been to four different schools told me, "My father doesn't respect me. I've messed up at school because I'm not a good student. But I have a lot of interests. I'm a good musician and I'm awfully good with my hands. I can make things and build things, but he doesn't respect me for any of these things that I do well." This is a very accurate self report. He was not a good student. He had not been serious about his schoolwork. His parents were very "A" oriented, and kept switching him from one private school to the next. He was, however, a very fine musician and he was indeed good with his hands. He was stating what he really needed from his folks. He was speaking from the heart. He was a very verbal, insightful young man. As we helped his parents be more respectful, his grades picked up a bit so that he was passing everything and getting some Bs.

His love, however, was music and with his family's support, he worked at it very hard.

2. *Recognize your limits.* Parents and the community at large often don't recognize their own limits. You have leverage with your teenager, but that leverage is limited. You can give or take away an allowance, access to the car, etc. You can give or take away respect and support. But you are really quite limited if a child decides to act out. You can't be there every second of every day. Teenagers have free time. They can have sex in the afternoon. They can drink in the afternoon. They can use drugs or hurt each other in the afternoon.

Because your control and leverage is limited, you have to rely on persuasion and cooperation. During the adolescent years, your relationship is shifting from one where you can be fairly autocratic (during the early and grade-school years) to one that is based on mutual respect and cooperation.

In using persuasion, the only way that your child will agree to your views is if you have a solid, nurturing, respectful relationship. If this isn't there, and you just try to enforce your opinions, your child is not likely to want to listen to your message. But if the closeness is there, if the respect is there, many teenagers will listen to reason. So if you recognize the limits of your power, you won't fall into the trap of getting angry and issuing orders that you cannot enforce. Advice to parents of adolescents has tended to go from one extreme to the other— toughness to indulgence. We have a hard time integrating these two. Support, respect, firmness, and guidance need to all work together.

3. *Reflective thinking.* Always attempt to increase an adolescent's ability for self-observation and reflection. There are millions of opportunities for this in a day. Your teenager wants to use the car. Instead of "Yes" or "No," explore what he wants to do, for how long, and whether or not his homework is done. Anytime you have this kind of discussion with someone, it helps him reflect on his own desires. Self-reflection is the gift

you give your child as he leaves home for work or college. As a society, that's the gift we give teenagers as they grow into adults and have to be responsible citizens. Those with self-reflection can solve problems and assess and evaluate their own impulses and desires. Those without this ability are caught in the here-and-now and limited to their immediate and often impulsive reactions to events.

Teenagers with learning and developmental problems require extra practice at self-reflection and problem-solving. Even those with severe difficulty can be helped. We worked with a group of teenagers and adults who were diagnosed as mentally retarded and some of whom had autistic patterns as well. In one situation, two young adults had decided to live together because they fell in love. On traditional IQ tests their scores were in the seventies. They were both working in a sheltered workshop and living in supervised housing. When they started coming late for work after being granted permission to live together, the staff said, "Well, obviously you are not responsible. You can't get to work on time. You'll have to go back to your own apartments, to your own rooms." There was no discussion. These kids were not given a chance to answer the question, "What happened? How come you can't get to work on time?" It turned out that one of them had motor planning problems and couldn't dress quickly and the other one was being nice and staying to help him. Rather than help them reflect by saying, "Well, do you think you are going to have to get up earlier?" or "Do you need an aide to help with dressing?" they were reacted to in a concrete, non-reflective way. After a consultation, the program tried the reflective approach and the couple decided to get up early and call for help if they needed it. It worked and they are doing well. More importantly, they learned that they could solve a problem themselves.

In addition to these three overriding principles, the methods we have described throughout this book—increased nurturing (hang-out time), problem-solving, empathy, small steps, and limits—will help an adolescent recognize and overcome feelings of insecurity.

With adolescents, however, these five steps need to be carried out with some additional caveats.

### Hang-Out Time

Hanging out with one's adolescent child (that is, "floor time" for adolescents) is just as important as with a grade-school child. Creating access for the adolescent is much more challenging, however. The adolescent tends to want to hang out, and appropriately so, with his own peers. Whereas in childhood it's a question of parents making time for children, often in adolescence it's a question of adolescents making time for parents. The shoe is now on the other foot.

One of the best ways of creating access is to get interested in things that your adolescent is interested in. He may go with you to that concert because you got the tickets or to watch Michael Jordan basketball because you have the seats or to his favorite restaurant because you are paying the bill (and his allowance already got spent this week).

Also, before adolescents learn to drive and get their licenses, most are dependent on parents for being driven places. They have many places they want to be driven to. Instead of resenting the chauffeur role, put on your "listening cap." Enjoy the ride. Catch up with your teenager and hear about what's on his mind. The key here, as with the grade-school child and even his preschool counterpart, is to follow the child's lead and talk, whether it's talking about music, friends, obnoxious teachers, or why you are driving so badly and how they will drive better than you once they get their license. Whatever the subject, follow their lead, help elaborate, and get a sense of what's cooking in the child's life. Demanding questions or intrusive pressures are unlikely to create the atmosphere you want. And even though you have a captive audience, lecturing will defeat the whole purpose of this time together.

## Problem-Solving

Here, too, look for those opportunities—whether it's driving somewhere or sharing a favorite activity, such as music or sports—that can create access. To help the teenager learn to anticipate difficult tasks ahead of time, talk about tomorrow, and visualize and picture the challenges that tomorrow will bring. This, however, requires a real collaboration.

If challenges come up, if there is a challenge with a coach, a drama teacher, or in a friendship (and many teenagers will use their very available parents to discuss these issues), it's a wonderful opportunity to do some anticipatory problem-solving with visualization as we described earlier in the chapter on grade-school children. When discussing colleges, for example, it's a perfect time to ask the adolescent to picture how it would feel in each college. What would the different atmospheres feel like? Problem-solving discussions won't happen each and every time you are hanging out, but they will happen some of the time.

## Empathy

Empathizing is difficult with adolescents because they require a larger range of empathy than younger children do. They may be involved in wanting to put a tattoo on a part of their body that you can't even contemplate, let alone empathize with. You may have to dig deep into your own adolescent experiences to imagine how awkward you felt and what means you used to feel more secure about your body. The tattoo may be a way to express individuality. It also could be a way to feel more attractive and exciting. While it's not what your generation thought about, it's what your child's generation is thinking about. That doesn't mean that you will go along with it if you feel that there are health risks, or even if you feel that it's risky because your child may change his mind in a few weeks. But if you want to help your child reason it through and become a more reflective person, you need to be able to empathize with his perspective and at the same time bring up other perspectives. For many adolescent issues, the range of empathy will require a great effort on a parent's part.


## Small Steps

With an academic or social challenge, or a challenge with being more disciplined, the key is not to expect miraculous change overnight. Try to get a sense of the steps that it would take for the teenager to master this particular area.

For example, let's say the challenge is to move from being isolated and hiding out in one's own home computer area to doing more things with peers and friends. This will generally not happen easily. The first step might be simply having more of a relationship with one's own father or one's own mother with enjoyable activities and conversation and through that interaction regenerate one's interest in people. From there, it may be that an activity involving other kids could be built around this core interest. For example, perhaps a class where new programming techniques were being developed would be appealing, where there would be other students who shared this interest. In this way, step-by-step, you can help a child move from one way of behaving to another that you, and perhaps they (although they may not admit it) feel is much more desirable. The idea is to break down the problem into many, many small steps and try to make gradual progress. Whenever you meet resistance at one level, break that step down into smaller and smaller steps so that eventually there is a sense of mastery.

In choosing the steps, make sure they are building blocks of the goal. For example, simply introducing the adolescent to others his age won't work well unless you first work on increasing the desire to have a relationship.

## Limit-Setting

Limit-setting is particularly difficult with adolescents because, as we said, you no longer have the control over your child's life that you did during earlier childhood. Many adolescents will soon be driving, spending a lot of time at friends' houses, and often going out in the evening (at least on weekends). How do you set limits and provide guidance in such a circumstance?

The first, and most critical, step is simply to recognize the fact that life has changed. For some parents, this fact is tremendously frustrating and upsetting. They try to create an illusion of control and get into power struggles and fights with their children. They become almost irrationally obsessed with controlling their children's behavior. When their children don't let them do so or rebel, the stakes go up higher and higher until there are severe family conflicts, sometimes involving physical fights between sons and fathers. It is at that point, often, that professional consultation is sought.

If parents can accept their own limits, they can take a second step—providing guidance and direction for their teenagers—which is more collaborative and has as its goal the teenager's developing internal standards and judgment. After all, eventually today's adolescents will be on their own, even taking care of us. The best thing we can give them is good judgment. Help children internalize values and ideals that will guide them even when a parent isn't there.

Before discussing how to achieve this, however, it should also be clear that while we are advocating being realistic about how much control one has over a teenager's life, it is also important not to shirk the day-to-day and moment-to-moment responsibilities that one does have in setting limits. For example, limits can be set in terms of curfews, access to cars, responsibility for getting home on time, and the like. One way of teaching responsibility is to have firm but reasonable expectations, not for attitudes but for actual behaviors. Some of these are still under the parents' control to some degree, and parents can take various measures when objectives are not being met. For example, a child who is not getting his homework done may not be allowed to watch the ballgame or spend hours on the telephone. Parents may have to hang in there helping with the homework or very closely supervising homework. The child gets a sense of the parents' willingness to be heavily involved with him around critical activities. He will usually go along with the parents' agenda if it's done warmly, supportively, and respectfully. Parents' concerns are conveyed not through power struggles or a temper tantrum on a parent's side and not through a fight, but through the willingness to put hours and hours of time in with that teenager to help him learn the skills he needs, whether they are academic or social.

But to return to the larger question of limit-setting in adolescents, how do you instill the internal judgment and values that can guide the teenager from the inside? In a few years, the child will be going off to college, to work, or elsewhere and will, in all likelihood, be living on his own. Your input will be even less at that time. Therefore, these are the precious few years to instill judgment and values. See this as a transition period during which you have to develop internal values and judgment through collaboration. In fact, you are setting the stage now for a lifelong collaboration. It's very helpful if grown children at all different ages can come back to their parents and draw on their greater experience and wisdom as well as challenge them (where the child's experiences may be more appropriate to a new task at hand).

Collaboration that can instill judgment and values comes about through the steps we've outlined above—caring, time together, discussions in which you anticipate challenges and brainstorm together, empathy for the adolescent's perspective, questions to encourage reflection, and support in taking small steps toward a difficult goal. These experiences offer the tools for having better and better judgment and applying it to new problems. In a relationship where the child has more positive than negative feelings toward parents, he will likely want to take in those values or ideals that he feels are consistent with his own goals.

No child should, or does, take in all the ideals or values of parents, but many children take in a surprisingly large amount. What they take in is often undetectable to the parent, however. For example, the child may disagree about a variety of issues ranging from politics, to choice of music, to friendships, to career choice, and even to religion. It looks like the child is really quite rejecting of both parents' values. However, if that child decides to have a family, just like mom and dad did; decides to nurture his children with warmth and commitment, like his parents did; and respects other people and empathizes with their needs, just like his parents do, he has learned and incorporated a great deal from his parents. He may have incorporated the values of the parents' religion without taking on their religious theology. He has gotten the essence of both parents' character without taking on the same interests as the parents. Most kids who are well nurtured by their families, even when their interests seem far removed from those of their parents, are actually more similar to their parents than either one often is prepared to acknowledge or even realize.

These five principles should be implemented at all times and be increased during times of insecurity and distress. This is the first line of family help. The principles allow for relationships that encourage openness and expressiveness. They often help the adolescent overcome some of the milder anxieties and facilitate good coping capacities for the future. However, if the distress is severe—for example, if the adolescent is very depressed—professional help may be needed. Similarly, if the worry didn't seem that great but it doesn't respond and the problem continues and is getting worse, professional consultation is indicated. But even during a professional consultation or evaluation and treatment program, it's these family processes that will create the context for learning to cope and grow emotionally. They create the secure base upon which an adolescent can progress into a stable and fulfilled adulthood.

# 6

# Helping Children and Adolescents Prepare for the Future

WE STATED EARLIER THAT WE CAN'T HAVE A SECURE child without a secure family. Similarly, a secure family requires a secure community, and a secure community needs to be part of a secure nation and world.

In the past, one could isolate a nation from its neighbors. But for many years now, the world has become much more interdependent: economically, politically, and, through modern communications, culturally. The tragedies of terrorism dramatize that "shared dangers" also make the world more interdependent.

Interdependency requires a new psychology that enables us to broaden our own sense of humanity and of responsibility. Only improved understanding and collaboration, coupled with wise long-term policies that consider the needs of others, can move us in this direction. Even effective military action will require this perspective. For example, effective limit-setting and military action in the future will be possible if the "outlaw" groups are kept to an absolute minimum through effective global collaboration. Such collaboration will mean we have to be much more concerned than we have been about the welfare of children, families, and communities around the globe. It will also mean preparing our own children to live in an interdependent future.

Secure children require special opportunities to broaden their sense of humanity and empathy. Parents and schools need to collaborate, and parents can influence this by participation in boards of education, PTAs, and other processes that influence policies in schools. During the adolescent years, children need to be learning to think cross culturally through exploring the way different people around the world experience and view life. Being knowledgeable about South American, European, Asian, and Middle Eastern cultures, as well as many others, will be critical for protecting the future of the world.

This will require much more culturally and psychologically based understanding than that currently available in typical history curriculums. An approach to understanding the world should include the studies of economics, sociology, politics, cultural anthropology, and psychology. Such integrated courses are not commonly available in most schools. They are, however, offered in a few internationally oriented schools. One such example is the geography curriculum at the Washington International School, which teaches a student body made up of children from all over the world. It has a wonderful, broad-based curriculum and teaches children about the world from multiple perspectives. Children who graduate from this program, as far as I can tell, have a broad intuitive and empathetic understanding of the perspectives of different peoples and cultures. Most high school or even college graduates don't learn to think this way.

In addition, parents and schools need to involve teenagers actively in policy discussions, practicing for the day when they become voting citizens. A lot of teenagers will have extreme views; it's best for you to hear about these, learn about their sources, and help them reason further. Also, educators and parents will have to focus not just on the intellectual foundations of empathy but also on its emotional foundations. The ability to understand others comes from being in relationships at school and at home where caring, nurturance, support, and extending one's horizons to the views of others are all part of the value system.

In our hustle and bustle world of achievement, we have lost sight of the basics that enable people to solve problems. Our schools and our families will need to embrace these more basic abilities. True empathy is not adopted at the expense of education; it fosters learning. To ensure understanding, which is what education is about, requires the ability to understand and use the experiences of others. These "others" may be from different time periods or cultures. They are also the children and adults of the future.

As parents we have a responsibility to help our children to acquire a broader comprehension of humanity and of the ecology of our planet than any other generation has had before. We can begin at home by setting in motion the experiences that will enable the adults of the future to work in and protect an interdependent world.

# INDEX

academics, grade-school problems,
92–93
active children, floor time, 69
adolescence, 141–150
changes at puberty, 87–88
development of empathy, 41–44,
145–146
facing challenges in, 146–147
hanging out time, 144–145
internal standards/self-sense, 40
limit setting, 147–149
nurturing, 141–142
overview of, 7
preparing for future, 151–153
privacy issues, 36
problem-solving skills, 28–30,
145
recognizing multiple causes, 38
reflective thinking skills, 32,
142–144
adolescence, new strengths in,
123–134
ability to learn, 131–132
anticipating future, 124–125
dealing with dependency,
125–127
delayed gratification, 131
growing self-sense, 123–124
intimacy issues, 132–134
mastering aggression, 129–131
sexuality, 128–129
adolescence, signs of distress in,
134–141
alcohol/drugs, 138
fear of future, 140–141
fears/worries/anxieties, 138–139
lack of relationships/interests,
134–136
obsessive interests, 136

overinvolvement in sexual
behavior, 137
preoccupation with one's own
body, 136–137
risk-taking behavior, 137
sadness/depression, 139
aggression
expressing with gestures, 24
expressing with words, 51–52
in floor time, 65–66
in adolescence, 129–131
insecurity and, 56, 100
alcohol use, in adolescence, 138
anger. see aggression; frustration
tolerance
assertiveness training
early childhood, passivity and,
59–60, 68
grade-school, floor time for, 108
grade-school, overly fearful
children, 91
grade-school, problem-solving
and, 113

babies. see infants
behavior
fragmented, 59
risk-taking, 56, 137
body posture, as expression of
feelings, 22–27

calm regulation, 45–46
collaboration
global interdependency and,
151–152
setting limits with adolescents
and, 148–149
competition, 83–86
conscience, development of, 88

155

# Acknowledgments

I want to thank Jan Tunney and Sue Morrison for their heroic efforts in helping prepare the manuscript for publication, and Sarah Miller for her extraordinary clinical support of the office. I want especially to thank Merloyd Lawrence for her guidance and, as usual, her gifted editing of the manuscript.

# ABOUT THE AUTHOR

Stanley I. Greenspan, M.D., is clinical professor of psychiatry and pediatrics at George Washington University Medical School and Chairman of the Interdisciplinary Council on Developmental and Learning Disorders. He is also a practicing child psychiatrist; founding president of Zero to Three: The National Center for Infants, Toddlers and Families; and a supervising child psychoanalyst at the Washington Psychoanalytic Institute. He has been director of the Mental Health Study Center and the Clinical Infant Development Program at the National Institute of Mental Health.

Dr. Greenspan, whose work guides the care of infants and children with developmental and emotional problems throughout the world, is the author or editor of more than 30 books and 100 articles. His many influential works, which have been translated into over a dozen languages, include *The Irreducible Needs of Children* (with T. Berry Brazelton, M.D.); *The Growth of the Mind* (with Beryl Lieff Benderly); *Building Healthy Minds*; *The Challenging Child*; *The Child with Special Needs* (with Serena Wieder, Ph.D.); and *The Four-Thirds Solution*.

Among Dr. Greenspan's many national honors are the American Psychiatric Association's Ittleson Prize, its highest award for child psychiatry research; the American Orthopsychiatry's Ittleson Prize for pioneering contributions to American mental health (he is the only individual to have received both Ittleson prizes); and the Edward A. Strecker Award for Outstanding Contributions to American Psychiatry. His work has been featured in the PBS *Nova* documentary, *Life's First Feelings*, and in *Newsweek*, the *New York Times*, and the *Washington Post*, as well as on NBC, ABC, and CBS national news and *Nightline*.